BREWER'S
·HANDBOOK·

Inspiring | Educating | Creating | Entertaining

Brimming with creative inspiration, how-to projects, and useful information to enrich your everyday life, Quarto Knows is a favorite destination for those pursuing their interests and passions. Visit our site and dig deeper with our books into your area of interest: Quarto Creates, Quarto Cooks, Quarto Homes, Quarto Lives, Quarto Drives, Quarto Explores, Quarto Gifts, or Quarto Kids.

This edition published in 2018 by Chartwell Books, Inc.
an imprint of The Quarto Group
142 West 36th Street, 4th Floor
New York, NY 10018 USA
T (212) 779-4972 F (212) 779-6058
www.QuartoKnows.com

Previously published as *Fearless Brewing* by
Brian Kunath (1998) and *The Brewer's Bible*
by Brian Kunath (2011)

This book was conceived, designed, and produced by
The Bright Press, an imprint of The Quarto Group
The Old Brewery
6 Blundell Street
London N7 9BH
United Kingdom

ISBN: 978-0-7858-3660-5
QTT.BREB2

Printed in China

10 9 8 7 6 5 4 3 2 1

Credits:
Consultant: Erik Lars Myers
Designer: Matt Windsor
Cover Designer: Greg Stalley
Project Editor: Jane Roe
Senior Editor: Caroline Elliker
Creative Director: James Evans
Associate Publisher: Emma Bastow
Publisher: Mark Searle

Image credits:
4, 29 (bottom): Benoit Daoust/Shutterstock;
9: Eviaphoto/Shutterstock; 10: Olga Niekrasova/
Shutterstock; 12, 28, 31: Joshua Rainey
Photography/Shutterstock; 13: David Tran Photo/
Shutterstock; 20: andrebanyai/Shutterstock; 27:
Phoenixns/Shutterstock; 29 (top): wavebreakmedia/
Shutterstock; 30: momente/Shutterstock; 33:
Vaclav Mach/Shutterstock; 49, 95 (bottom): Hans
Geel/Shutterstock; 53, 73: Ramon L. Farinos/
Shutterstock; 62: Hugh K. Telleria/Shutterstock;
93: LacekL/Shutterstock; 98: Anze Furlan; 113:
Kristen Prahl/Shutterstock; 114: SeventyFour/
Shutterstock; 133: Alp Aksoy/Shutterstock;
135: Chad Springer/Getty Images; 140: Deyan
Georgiev/Shutterstock; 163: Kantapit Tanadkarn/
Shutterstock; 175: Heavenman/Shutterstock;
186: g-stockstudio/Shutterstock; 190: JHK2303;
192: Wollertz/Shutterstock; 195: Rawpixel.com/
Shutterstock; 212 Alizada Studios/Shutterstock.

Chartwell Books titles are also available at discount for retail, wholesale, promotional, and bulk purchase. For details, contact the Special Sales Manager by email at specialsales@quarto.com or by mail at The Quarto Group, Attn: Special Sales Manager, 401 Second Avenue North, Suite 310, Minneapolis, MN 55401, USA.

BREWER'S
· HANDBOOK ·

How to Brew Delicious Beers at Home

BRIAN KUNATH

CHARTWELL
BOOKS

CONTENTS

◄ INTRODUCTION

"I think something exploded in your room."
If you made a list of things you don't want to hear upon arriving home, this has to crack the top ten. Yet these were the words delivered to me by my roommate one humid summer evening in 1994. Let me explain. You see, I'm a homebrewer. And back in 1994, I wasn't a very good one.

That tragic batch, henceforth to be named "Exploding Irish Stout," had felt like it was going to be a winner. But halfway through bottling the stuff, I'd run out of sanitized beer bottles. No problem. I pinched off the transfer hose and hastily washed out some wine bottles—the cheap fortified stuff you buy when you're broke and twenty-three. Into my bedroom closet the bottles went, lined up like soldiers standing in formation.

Five days later, they exploded. Looking back, it was probably some combination of over-priming and cheap bottles that took out the batch, laminating the inside of my closet with a sticky amber film that held bits of shattered glass like diamonds against the wallpaper. But it shook my confidence and forced me to confront my middling success as a homebrewer.

What had gone wrong? Why couldn't I get consistent results? How do you get malt extract out of wallpaper? I couldn't answer any of these questions. In fact, I knew little about how to brew beer except that you put

some ingredients in a pot and mixed. I bought a bunch of books on homebrewing. I wanted to understand how malt, hops, water, and yeast conspire to transform sweet liquid into magical beer. The more I read, I realized that while the science of brewing is very complex, the craft is fairly simple and straightforward.

This is a book that addresses the mistakes I made as a novice homebrewer. Each of the suggestions I initially ignored in other texts are stressed in this book. There are four basic concepts that, if understood and followed, will ensure great beer.

These are:
1. Maintaining sanitary conditions
2. Following proper procedure
3. Keeping a detailed journal for each batch of homebrew
4. Understanding the art and science of brewing

This book explores each of these ideas and offers a bit more. There is a chapter that details cleaning and sanitation of your equipment and work area. I have included guidance on making Extract Homebrew Worksheets to organize each batch of beer

you brew, and to help you predict how your homebrew will turn out. These charts serve as a map and a journal. I recommend that a notebook and a calculator be used in conjunction with the charts, or you can download a brewing app (but keep it simple, for now). There are also sections that delve lightly into the science behind brewing to help you understand what is going on in the brewpot.

I have tried to write a book that will lure the curious, calm the clueless, and quickly guide the novice toward intermediate procedures and, more importantly, great homebrew. So whether you like Porter or Pilsner, Weizen or Witbier, or Bock or Barley Wine, fear not. Successful brewing is right around the corner.

A STYLISH HISTORY

Geography, trade, economics, and climate have all influenced the development of beer. In one form or another, beer has existed for more than 8,000 years. As with the adaptive nature of human beings, beer has changed with the climate. And as people have forged civilizations, established trade routes, and made technological advancements, beer has always been close at hand, mirroring our evolution.

Beer has been both scion of scientific discovery and patron to its progress. For example, Louis Pasteur was studying the causes of beer spoilage in the mid-nineteenth century. He found that during brewing, in wort (unfermented beer) that was raised

to a boil and then cooled quickly, a great number of microorganisms would be eliminated. Thus, he increased the shelf life of beer. This process was tested in the dairy industry with great success. Where untreated milk soured, harboring bacteria that caused typhoid and tuberculosis, pasteurized milk was safe. Historically, new medicines and inventions have often resulted from the work of men and women striving toward unrelated goals. If serendipity has played a part in the progressive application of scientific inquiry, then it is fitting that the "invention" of beer probably came as a desperate experiment to remedy an accident.

▲ Beer has long been part of civilization, as this preserved brewery from ancient China shows.

▲ With the rise of the craft beer revolution has come a seemingly infinite number of new beers and breweries. There are over 7,000 breweries in the US alone.

ORIGINS

Most likely, an ancient Sumerian farmer left a crop of cut barley out in a rainstorm. In an effort to save his resource from rot, he may have laid the grain out in the sun to dry. By exposing the barley to water and then allowing it to dry under the hot Mesopotamian sun, this farmer would have produced "malt." Upon tasting the barley, he would have found it sweeter and easier to chew. A gruel or bread made with malt would taste better than that made with raw barley, as hard starches within the grain are converted into sugars as malt is produced. Soon, or perhaps much later, a bread or cake made of malted barley may have been exposed to further rainwater. This wet mixture may then have been host to airborne wild yeasts. Fermentation would result, and any liquid squeezed from the bread would be beer. That meant beer was viewed as a natural product composed of elements from both sky and earth. Indeed, early civilizations credited spiritual, not scientific, sources for their beer.

The Sumerian goddess of beer was called Ninkasi: "The lady who fills the mouth." Egyptian hieroglyphics depict the process of brewing as early as the Fifth Dynasty. Their gods of brewing and beer were Hathor and Seth. The Romans, who regarded beer as an inferior beverage, still bestowed respect for the "grain wine." While Bacchus was praised as the god of wine, Ceres, the goddess of agriculture, was said to impart her strength (in Latin, *vis*) upon those who drank beer.

Just when mankind stumbled upon the fermented barley beverage remains a mystery. Shards of pottery dating from 3500–3100 BCE have been excavated from sites in Iraq. Grooves within some of these remnants have

▲ The entrance to the Orval Abbey in Belgium, one of the eleven Trappist breweries in the world.

been found to contain the hardened residue of beer. The use of such pitchers, along with other empirical data, suggests that beer was already a dietary staple among the people of Mesopotamia. Clay tablets found in the same region depict groups of people drinking beer from a pitcher through long straws forged from gold. These tablets have been dated to 4000 BCE.

Archaeologists have traced the study of various types of barley as far back as 6000 BCE. This would indicate a fairly sophisticated understanding of the grain. In fact most historians believe that barley was being used for the production of bread and/or beer 2,000–3,000 years prior to this.

EARLY BREWERS

In most ancient societies, the lofty task of brewing beer was bestowed upon women. Sumerian and Babylonian priestesses were the only people allowed to brew. In Egypt the woman of the house directed the brewing process. Egyptian women created many styles of beer that were rationed to workers, and even exported. The Vikings also gave the task of brewing to women. Both men and women drank heavily in this society. The nomadic Norsemen brought beer to each land they terrorized and plundered. The Vikings believed that after death they would enter Valhalla, where Odin (or Woden) would entertain them with tales of battles during long drinking sessions.

EUROPEAN BREWING

The influence of earlier societies seeped into Europe. The Anglo-Saxons settled into northern Europe after the Romans withdrew. A large variety of fermented beverages sated the appetites of the nomadic Anglo-Saxons. They used whatever was available—grains, honey, bog myrtle (sweet gale), and a host of other herbs and spices. One popular drink was mead, a honey-fermented, spiced beverage.

Malted barley was used as the chief ingredient of beer in many parts of Europe. Records show that hops, previously a flavoring additive among many other herbs and spices, was used with some consistency in Bavarian beer after the eighth century CE. After the Norman Conquest, Europe became united under the Roman Catholic Church. The Church quickly regulated the production of beer. Monks were allowed to brew, first for personal consumption, and later to support the abbeys. The erudite monks refined brewing practices. In fact, it may have been the monks who first started using hops regularly as a preservative in ale. While they praised God for the magic transformation of wort into beer, they understood that the hop plant helped to stabilize beer, and thus applied early science to brewing.

EARLY LAGERS

Up until the fifteenth century, all beers produced were ales. Since ales are fermented at a relatively warm temperature, they are susceptible to bacterial contaminants, which also favor warm temperatures. Since little was known of microbiology, brewers had to learn or experience empirically that brewing in the summer (when airborne wild yeasts and bacteria are at high levels) was a dicey prospect. Therefore, most brewing took place during the fall and winter months.

Bavarians in the 1400s began creating lager beer by placing fermentation vessels in the cold caves of the Alps in early March. They soon realized that the beer could be stored safely throughout the summer, and into the fall when the last reserves were drunk during a festival in October. These early lagers may have hosted strains of yeast that could function at very low temperatures. Since these yeast strains could thrive at temperatures as low as 34°F (1°C), the beer would ferment. Lees (yeast sediment) taken from these batches may have been the first "cultivated" lager yeast.

▲ **A medieval tin beer mug—until the fifteenth century, all beers were ales.**

▲ Fermenters and brite tank inside of a small craft brewery.

QUALITY CONTROL

The next milestone in European brewing came in 1516, when Bavaria enacted the Reinheitsgebot—a purity law designed to protect the consumer from overpricing and poorly crafted beer. The law stated that the only ingredients allowed to be used for the brewing of beer were barley, hops, and water. Some German brewers stick to the archaic code to this day, despite competition from mass-produced, high-adjunct lager imports.

SCIENCE SOOTHES THE WILD YEAST

In the 1800s, a German scientist, Theodore Schwann, armed with a microscope, proposed that yeast fermentation was a living process. Pasteur later confirmed this observation. Fermentation was indeed the work of living microorganisms, much like the bacteria that feed off meat and milk. Science had uncovered what had been a mystery for millennia. The proof was in the pasteurization. Now, like fire that was stolen from the gods by Prometheus and given to mankind, the magical fermentation process was no longer the product of divine hands but something that humans could control.

In the late 1800s, the Danish scientist Emil Hansen isolated two important strains of yeast. The first was *Saccharomyces cerevisiae*, the ale yeast that had been used for up to 10,000 years. The other was *Saccharomyces pastorianus* (originally *S. carlsbergensis*, named after the Carlsberg brewery in Denmark where it was first identified). This major scientific leap improved methods of brewing enormously.

THE REVOLUTION

While Prohibition had effectively snuffed out most regional breweries in the United States, Britain was slowly being taken over by large breweries that economically bullied local taverns into using their products. After Prohibition ended in America, large breweries produced light lagers almost exclusively. The two countries faced a similar dilemma. Some British citizens formed a consumer organization called CAMRA (the Campaign for Real Ale), which promoted homebrewing as a reaction against the "big six" breweries who had invaded local pubs. Americans began homebrewing in the 1970s, once students returning from European tours realized that there was an enormous variety of quality beer available in other countries. In 1979, Congress legalized homebrewing in the US. Around the same time, the homebrew pioneer Charlie Papazian created the American Homebrewers' Association, a nonprofit organization that educates homebrewers on the latest techniques.

THE REBIRTH OF TRADITION

During the past few decades, beer has enjoyed a renaissance. No longer a homogenous drink imbibed by the "unsophisticated," beer is rightfully taking its place next to wine as a versatile, complex, and delicious beverage. Microbreweries and brewpubs across America have revived old and forgotten recipes from around the world. Today, there are more than a million people homebrewing in the United States alone. In Britain CAMRA has succeeded in bringing real "cask-conditioned" ale back into local pubs. The brewing revolution is stronger than ever. Men and women who began as homebrewers head many small breweries. There is a wonderful synergy between microbrewers and homebrewers. The former offer an array of quality beer for the hobbyist to sample and emulate. To use an appropriate metaphor, these breweries provide grist for the mill. In turn, many homebrewers are inspired to refine their craft, perhaps even aspiring toward professional brewing. All of this activity has ignited the creativity of millions. Who knows where the next style will come from?

▲ A bright, beautiful snifter of craft beer.

BEERS OF THE WORLD

The following is a listing of many major beer styles. While most countries of the world produce beer in some form, this list concentrates on beer produced in Europe and North America.

ALES

Ales are made with ale yeast (*Saccharomyces cerivisiae*), which ferments wort at a warm temperature and creates distinctive fruit characteristics or "esters." Many of these help define certain styles of ale.

BELGIUM

BELGIAN PALE Similar to an English pale ale, but the malt profile is more complex due to the candi sugar and other additives. Also, Belgian pales are hopped at a lower rate, highlighting soft fruit notes.

FLANDERS RED This is a very tart, light- to medium-bodied ale, often fermented with multiple yeast strains. Vienna malt provides the color. Belgian red is often aged in uncoated oak tuns for up to two years. Hopping rates are low.

BELGIAN STRONG ALE There are light and dark varieties of this ale, which runs from a pale amber to burgundy and even a deep brown color. These are potent, heavily malted beers with low hopping rates. Strong ales are colored with candi sugar, which can produce vinous notes, along with a warming sensation on the tongue, associated with the high alcohol content.

FARO This lambic is sweetened after fermentation with sugar and/or caramel. Faro retains the trademark sour flavor of a lambic, but a subtle sweetness and a soft, rounded palate subdue this.

FLANDERS BROWN The color of this ale is copper to brown. There is a slight tartness, along with a fruity, spicy palate. Bitterness is low to medium, with no hop aroma or flavor.

FRAMBOISE This is a raspberry-flavored lambic, dominated by an intensely tart aroma and flavor.

GUEUZE This very dry lambic is the product of old and young blends. It is very pale in color with a complex, musty flavor and some acidic tartness.

LAMBIC These famous ales are produced in the Senne Valley, where indigenous wild yeasts settle on the wort from open slats in the brewery roof. The result is an intense, sour beer. Lambic is made from malted barley and up to 40 percent unmalted wheat. Stale hops are used to help stabilize the beer without imparting bitterness, flavor, or aroma. Lambics are pale in color with some cloudiness.

TRAPPIST ALES These ales can be called Trappist only in the eleven monasteries where they are brewed. Six of these breweries—brewing the beers Orval, Chimay, Westmalle, Achel, Rochefort, and Westvleteren—are in Belgium. The others are located in the Netherlands (La Trappe and Zundert), Austria (Engelszell), Italy (Tre Fontane), and the US (St. Joseph's). These highly esteemed ales come in three styles. The house beer (or Patersbier) has the lightest body. The dubbel has a medium to full body, and a color ranging from copper to brown. The flavor is sweet and caramelly. The tripel is gold in color and is normally quite alcoholic, disproving those who associate dark color with alcoholic strength.

WIT OR WHITE This ale comprises malted barley and unmalted wheat. Witbier is pale and cloudy, and is often spiced with orange peel and coriander. Some estery flavors are acceptable. Hopping rates are low to medium.

▲ Gueuze, a very dry blended lambic.

◀ Kriek (cherry lambic).

15

THE BRITISH ISLES

BARLEY WINE The name comes from the winelike alcoholic potency, not the flavor. Barley wines have an immense malt profile. The sweetness is often matched by high hopping rates, although the malt character traditionally dominates. The color of this ale ranges from amber to copper. Fruity notes reminiscent of figs, prunes, or raisins may be apparent alongside caramel or toffee-like flavors. Unlike most ales, barley wine improves dramatically with age due to its alcohol content.

BITTER This self-descriptive beer actually overlaps somewhat in style with English pale ale. The color is golden to copper, with a light to medium body. The lower malt flavor may be outbalanced by higher hopping rates, but never at the expense of drinkability. Cask-conditioned bitters have the lower carbonation that is a characteristic of this storage and serving method.

▲ Bitter.

BROWN ALE British brown ale and British mild both fall in this category. Brown ale is sweet and full-bodied, with low hop bitterness and aroma. The mild is a lighter-bodied version of the brown.

IPA India pale ale was a beer originally drunk by English colonists in India. Though originally produced in London, the hard waters of Burton upon Trent proved a more favorable match to the heavy hop additions. Current British IPAs vary greatly in style, being anything from pale golden, low-potency beers to copper-brown, strong, and hoppy ales.

PALE ALE This classic ale is considered pale only in relation to milds, porters, and stouts. Pale ale is actually reddish to copper in color. Similar to bitter ale, pales are well-hopped, though more robust and complex, with fruit notes and hop character that vary among brands.

PORTER Originally called "entire," porters were traditionally aged in wooden vats before release. Today porter is characterized by a deep brown color with perhaps a tinge of amber if held against a light source. Generally, porters should be full-bodied with a malty sweetness balanced by a sharp bitterness of black malt. Hopping rates range from medium to high, but hop aroma or flavor should not dominate. Flavors like coffee, chocolate, or dark fruits may further characterize the modern porter.

SCOTTISH ALES These are a loose interpretation of the bitter to be found elsewhere in Britain. However, as the cold climate in Scotland hinders hop cultivation, the emphasis is on malt characteristics. Light Scottish ales are gold to amber in color, medium-bodied, and lightly hopped. Scottish "heavy" ales tend to be darker, richer ales, with emphasis on malt complexity. As low-hopped ales, they exhibit more pronounced notes of fruit and butterscotch. Scottish exports are heavier still, while retaining the characteristics of the Scottish heavy. Scotch ale, also known as "wee heavy," is typically more potent than other Scottish ales in general, and is often served in smaller glassware. The malt profile is very complex, exhibiting distinct notes of fruit and butterscotch on the palate.

STOUT A direct descendant of the porter, stouts retain many of its characteristics but add specialty malts, more hops, and various other ingredients that put this style in a class of its own. The name implies a big, hearty beer, but this moniker might better serve to illustrate the wide variance of substyles that exist within the general category. Ingredients ranging from whey and milk sugar to molasses and even oysters have been added. Stouts may be divided into three categories:

▲ Dry stout.

Dry stout was perfected in Ireland, and continues to be its premier export. Dry stouts tend to be black and opaque. The flavor is due to roasted unmalted barley, which offsets sweetness of malt additions. High-bittering hop rates provide balance; however, there is no hop flavor or aroma. The overall flavor starts with sweetness and finishes with dry coffee-like flavors.

Sweet stout is sweeter and fuller-bodied than its dry cousin due to decreased unmalted grain additions, as well as the introduction of lactose, chocolate malt, and sometimes flaked oats. The color and hop bitterness are the same as in dry stout.

Imperial stout came about because of a trade contract between eighteenth-century England and the Russian court. English breweries made stouts for the court but had to prepare the brew for a long journey. Thus, they crafted a high-gravity, highly hopped brew. The brew would complete fermentation en route, and the hops served to protect the beer from developing containments. The result was a huge brew; full-bodied, pitch black, highly alcoholic, and rich with fruity esters and hop flavor and aroma.

STRONG ALE/ENGLISH OLD ALE The name "old ale" originally designated mild ales that had been aged in oak barrels for a year or more, and "strong ale" describes the result. Prolonged maturation may boost alcoholic potency, "strengthening" these dark, rich ales. Fruity, estery notes are evident, along with rich caramel and toffee notes. While these ales are moderately hopped, it is the complex malt profile and warming potency that lingers on the tongue.

FRANCE

BIÈRE DE GARDE These ales are produced in northern France. Several malts and a long maturation (the name means "beer for keeping") in cellars produce a smooth, rich fruity beer. Bière de Garde is typically corked rather than capped. The color ranges from golden to a reddish brown. The flavor and aromatic notes vary, but the long cellaring that is typical provides a noticeable warming on the palate.

BIÈRE DE MARS Traditionally this ale was brewed in late fall using malt from the Champagne region of France, to be ready in March to celebrate the arrival of spring. These blond ales are malty and potent, yet smooth on the palate.

GERMANY

ALT In German, Altbier means old beer, a designation for ales that have been fermented at warm temperatures using top-fermenting yeast and lagered at cold temperatures for extended periods. The cold storage minimizes the production of esters. While alt may have some fruitiness, moderate hopping rates impart a good portion of the flavor profile.

DUNKELWEIZEN The name means literally "dark wheat," and these use dark malt to achieve a deep copper color. Wheat is also used, along with a special yeast strain that produces notes of banana and clove. Low hopping rates make this a smooth, sweet brew with an interesting finish.

HEFEWEIZEN As with most German wheat beers, these are produced in southern Germany. The combination of malted barley and wheat results in a light, cloudy ale with clove and banana aromas dominating the nose and palate. These beers leave yeast sediment at the bottom of the bottle. Devotees swirl the bottle, bringing added complexity to the flavor and mouth-feel.

KRISTALLWEIZEN These beers are similar to Hefeweizen, but they are filtered to remove the yeast. Again, wheat is used, up to 60 percent of the grain. These ales range in color, but all are highly carbonated and crystal-clear. Special yeast strains impart fruit and spice.

WEIZENBOCK Bocks are typically dark, potent lagers, but this variant is fermented with ale yeast. Weizenbock is typically darker than other German wheat beers, and is higher in alcohol.

◀ Bière de Mars.

▶ Bière de Garde.

NORTH AMERICA

While light lagers dominate the American market, craft breweries are reviving some European recipes with an American stamp. Hops from the Pacific northwest, as well as American-grown grains, are often favored by microbreweries for the unique qualities they lend to traditional styles of beer. The American brewers' love affair with the aromatic Cascade hop, for example, has been proven by its use in some American interpretations of European styles. More recent developments in hop breeding have seen new varieties that push the envelope of American craft brewing.

AMERICAN AMBER This moniker is rapidly becoming a designation for any medium-bodied beer that encompasses various shades of red. Estery and balanced with bittering and aromatic hops.

AMERICAN BROWN Unlike their milder British counterparts, American browns tend to favor higher alcohol content, less malt influence, and more hops.

AMERICAN CREAM ALE This is a unique American style. Cream ale is fermented at a warm temperature and then aged cold like a lager. Cream ale is generally light-bodied and golden in color. Hopping rates are low.

AMERICAN DOUBLE IPA As the name implies, this is the big brother of the American IPA (see above). A stronger, more malty, version of the IPA style, with appropriately excessive use of bittering and aroma hops to maintain an illusion of balance.

AMERICAN IPA Maltier, richer, and more potent than the American pale ale (see below), these ales are enormously popular in the US. Caramel notes initially coat the palate, but are ultimately dominated by a clean, bitter finish, crowned by the piney and citrusy characteristics of American-grown hops. This American interpretation is perhaps closer in spirit to the original IPA than contemporary British representatives, which sacrifice alcoholic power and hop character for easy drinkability.

AMERICAN PALE ALE These ales are drier than the British style, favoring American hop qualities. The color ranges from a light straw to red-brown.

AMERICAN WHEAT Several micro-breweries produce light ales of malted barley and wheat. Some bottle-condition their beer, leaving the yeast sediment characteristic of Hefeweizen, while others filter to a sparkling gold.

LAGER

Lagers are made with lager yeast (*Saccharomyces pastorianus*) which ferments wort at a cooler temperature, producing a very clean beer that can show off base ingredients a little better than ales. Because lager yeast also produces a bit of sulfur during fermentation, these beers tend to feel very dry and crisp while drinking.

AUSTRIA

VIENNA The famous Austrian brewer, Anton Dreher, created this lager in the mid-nineteenth century. During Austria's brief empire in Mexico, the style gained in popularity and continues to be made in Mexico, but has mostly faded from the market elsewhere. It ranges in color from amber to deep copper. This beer has a medium body, with moderate notes of toasted malt on the palate, and a low to medium hop flavor and aroma.

CZECH REPUBLIC

BOHEMIAN PILSNER In 1842, in a small brewery in Plzen (or Pilsen), Josef Groll created a revolutionary style of beer. The soft waters around Plzen perfectly matched the gentle flavor and aromatics of the indigenous Saaz hop and a new malting technique created a light, sweet maltiness unknown at that point in history. Traditional Bohemian Pilsners are light- to medium-bodied, have a smooth malty flavor, and are balanced by noble bittering hops.

▶ Pilsner.

◀ American IPA.

GERMANY

Traditional bock bread and beer share many characteristics. Hence, beer is often referred to as "liquid bread" and this phrase may have its derivation in the abbeys of Europe. Bock is a rich, malty brew that was consumed by fasting monks as a source of liquid nutrition. Bock is loaded with the sugars and carbohydrates that make up its sweet malt profile. Hops are used to balance the malt, but bitterness, hop flavor, and hop aroma are low. It may have a slight chocolate flavor, as well as caramel undertones.

DOPPELBOCK Stronger versions of the traditional bock, these lagers are full-bodied, and are sweet, and complex with notes of rich, dark fruit.

DORTMUNDER Originally brewed in hard-water regions of Dortmund, this lager is full-bodied, and sweeter and less hoppy than German Pilsner.

EISBOCK These Doppelbocks have been cooled to freezing, after which the frozen water is removed, resulting in a more potent brew. These taste similar to Doppelbocks, with added warmth due to the increased alcohol.

GERMAN PILSNER This lager is brewed all over Germany and its characteristics vary slightly from brewery to brewery. Generally, these are lighter versions of the Bohemian Pilsner. More emphasis is placed on hops, resulting in a drier beer with a floral aroma and finish.

HELLES BOCK These bocks are lighter in color than traditional bocks, but they retain most of the characteristics. The color ranges from pale to light amber. They also lack chocolate character.

MUNICH DUNKEL This is a dark, medium-bodied lager that is sweet, with notes of caramel and chocolate. Hops balance the malt but do not contribute aroma or flavor.

MUNICH HELLES This lager was brewed in response to the popularity of Pilsners in the 1920s. While the two styles share their color, Munich Helles are maltier, fuller-bodied, and less hoppy.

RAUCHBIER The name means "smoke beer," which describes the resultant flavor of drying malt over an oak or beechwood fire. This is a full-bodied lager with a sweetness that lurks beneath the aggressive smoky flavor and aroma. The color is copper to dark brown, and hopping rates are low to moderate.

SCHWARZBIER This dark-brown to black beer has a rough-around-the-edges malt flavor. While this medium-bodied lager provides some sweetness and chocolate flavors, these are crossed with the bitterness of added roasted malt.

NORTH AMERICA

AMERICAN BOCK/DARK While these are two different beers, their profiles are almost identical. Color alone differentiates these two styles, and color also distinguishes them from other American lagers. Each is light-bodied, has little or no perceivable hop aroma or flavor, and is darkened by specialty malts or caramel syrup.

AMERICAN DRY This light-bodied, effervescent lager uses genetically engineered yeast strains. American dry lager has little perceptible malt or hop flavor or aroma. The dry style is also popular in the Far East, notably Japan.

AMERICAN ICE This lager is frozen before filtration, resulting in a beer with more alcohol content. These beers are brewed with fewer adjuncts than most American lagers, and therefore the body is heavier. Hop aromas and flavor are very low.

AMERICAN LIGHT By law, these lagers must contain 25 percent fewer calories than standard lagers of the same brand. The body and carbonation is comparable to seltzer water. These beers have no malt or hop flavor.

AMERICAN PREMIUM/STANDARD Both of these lagers lack significant malt flavor or aroma. Hops are low. While American standards use a high level of adjuncts, American premium typically uses fewer.

CALIFORNIA COMMON BEER "Steam" beer developed in the late 1800s in California. When the Anchor Brewing Company of San Francisco put a trademark on the term "steam," California common was named to circumvent infringement. These beers use lager yeast at ale temperatures. Further maturation at warm temperatures produces a beer that is quite unlike most American lagers. Generally, these are medium-bodied, amber-colored, with a high hop bitterness and flavor.

MALT LIQUOR In some parts of the United States, these beers exceed legal alcohol limits that would allow them to be labeled beer, so US law requires that they must use this moniker.

▶ American dry.

◀ Munich Dunkel.

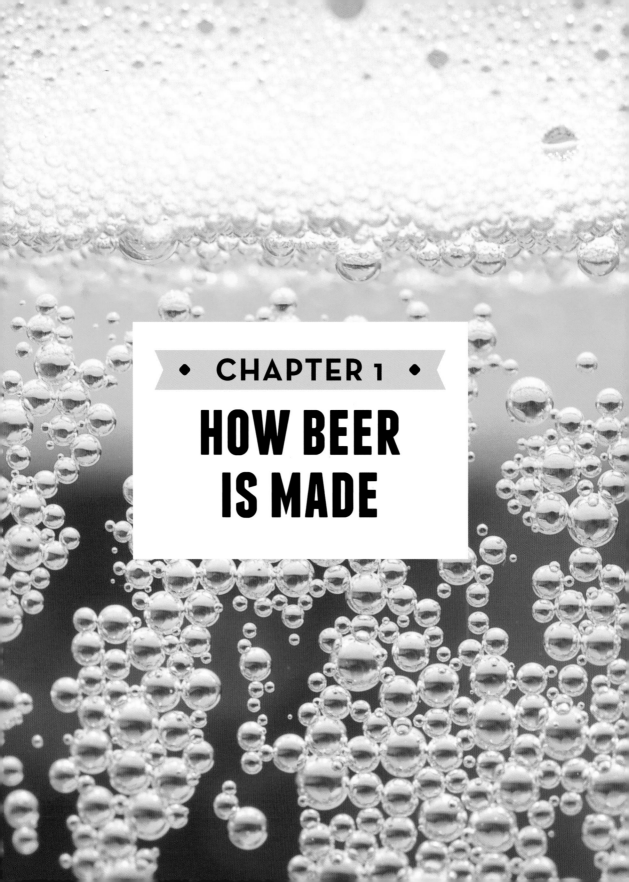

CHAPTER 1

HOW BEER IS MADE

AN ELEGANT MARRIAGE OF INGREDIENTS

Beer is composed of four main ingredients: malt, hops, yeast, and water. Malt is responsible for supplying much of the flavor, color, and texture of beer. Malt also provides a food supply for the yeast during brewing. Hops provide bitterness to balance the sweet sugars in the malt. The cone-shaped flower also adds aroma and flavor, and even helps to stabilize and preserve the flavor of beer. Yeast (used as a plural noun by many brewers) convert sugars from the malt into alcohol and carbon dioxide through a natural process called fermentation. Water is the vehicle through which all of the ingredients interact.

Furthermore, other ingredients may be added to achieve certain characteristics. Adjuncts (any source of sugar that is not malted barley) and other additives can be used to augment flavor, alter color, or help make beer clearer.

These are the elements that mix, mingle, and interact to form limitless varieties of ale and lager. Armed with the proper equipment, it is the brewmaster who is responsible for the orchestration of the ingredients.

Professional brewers and homebrewers share a common goal: to make a quality brew.

PROFESSIONAL BREWING

The last few decades have seen a huge increase in small-volume brewing, sometimes referred to as the craft brewing movement. The blend of different malts and hops is particular to each brewery, and also to each beer that it makes. At every stage, the head brewer is involved in selecting ingredients and developing recipes, ensuring that these are produced in a consistent manner. But one thing that people rarely talk about is perhaps the most important—the internal cleanliness of the brewery.

SANITATION

At every level of brewing, sanitation is key. All tanks, lines, fittings, and filters must be free of bacteria and yeast.

To achieve this, the head brewer at your local brewery uses caustics, heat, and acids. All the great recipes in the world will come to nothing without good sanitation practices. Once the equipment is clean and sanitary, ingredients are prepared.

MASHING

Whole grain malt must be gently cracked in a mill prior to use or purchased precrushed. This allows internal starches, dextrins, and sugars exposure to the brew water (known as "liquor"), while keeping the husks intact (useful later as a filter bed). All material is collected and transferred to the mash/lauter tun (or MLT).

The MLT is filled with a mixture of grain and hot water, heated to a temperature of 149–154°F (65–68°C), depending on the character of beer being brewed. At this point mineral salts may be added to adjust the water chemistry. This procedure is known as "mashing in." This mixture is stirred, and then left to rest at a temperature in the above range for about an hour. Care is taken to maintain a constant temperature. If too hot, starch-converting enzymes "die" (denature), resulting in a poorly fermentable wort.

During this time, starches are broken down into usable compounds—fermentable sugars. An iodine test determines when this conversion is complete. A sample from the MLT is placed on a plate and iodine dripped over. If it turns purple, starch is present and mashing must continue. If no color change occurs, mashing is complete. This resulting mixture of sweet malt sugar and "liquor" is called wort.

MASH-OUT, VORLAUF, AND LAUTERING

Once starch conversion is complete, the temperature may be raised to 169°F (76°C) to denature active enzymes, known as "mashing out."

After the mash-out, the head brewer begins the vorlauf. Fixed to the bottom of the MLT is a screen. The purpose is to allow the flow of wort through a valve under the screen, while retaining the husk material. Here the husks play a vital role as a filter bed. The wort is inspected for clarity and, if necessary, pumped back into the top of the MLT. This recirculation of wort through the grain bed until it is clear is called vorlaufing (Vorlauf is German for "fore-run" or first runnings). The wort is recirculated through the MLT until the wort runs clear and the grain forms a gently compacted bed. Once this is accomplished, lautering may begin.

Lautering is the process of draining clear wort from the mash. Wort is run from the MLT to the brew kettle. When the level of wort is almost down to the top of the filter bed, hot water (140–150°F/60–65°C) is added to rinse sugars from the grain in a process known as sparging. Care is taken to maintain a steady flow of sparge water so as not to compact the spongy filter bed, which would restrict a steady flow into the kettle. Once the kettle is filled to the proper level, the inlet valve is closed and boiling begins.

▲ Each of these beers uses different malts to achieve different colors, flavors, and textures.

BOILING

The contents of the kettle are boiled. Ideally, a steam jacket is the heat source, as this prevents scorching by offering an even supply of heat. During the first 5 minutes of the boil, proteins are precipitated out of the solution. Known as the hot break, this can cause foaming which, if left, could cause a boil-over. Once the wort settles into a rolling boil, hops are added in stages.

At the start of the boil, the hops create bitterness because they receive a longer boil time, which converts the alpha acids into bitterness, through a process known as "isomerization." Later hops contribute some bitterness and flavor to the brew. The final addition can come just minutes before the end of the boil, and these late hops impart flavor and, significantly, aroma.

Once the boil is completed (60–90 minutes) the heat is turned off. Boiled wort contains a lot of material that would harm the quality of the finished beer, and so the clear wort must be drawn off this sediment. This is achieved by whirlpooling the wort using circulation pumps. The act of whirlpooling drives solid material (known as trub, pronounced "troob") into the center of the vessle. When the wort is eventually pumped out, it is from a valve that sits higher than the collected sediment, avoiding the removal of trub. At this point, a sample of wort is drawn off and a reading taken to determine the concentration of sugars or the "gravity," with a floating hydrometer, or refractometer.

▼ It is said that brewery work is 10 percent brewing beer and 90 percent cleaning.

COOLING IN

The brewery uses a heat exchanger to quickly drop the temperature of the near-boiling wort to about 65°F (18°C). The heat exchanger transfers the heat from the hot wort into cold water. The wort runs through a long network of copper piping that makes contact with parallel piping holding cold water, quickly cooling the wort to proper temperatures through conduction.

Also, as the cooled wort enters the fermenter, it is oxygenated. Oxygen is vital for yeast growth and reproduction. The wort may be oxygenated sprayed in the fermenter, or may receive oxygen through an aeration stone.

PITCHING AND FERMENTATION

The cooled wort is ready for yeast. The yeast is added (or "pitched," as brewers say) to the cooled wort, ideally at around 65°F (18°C). The wort ferments under a carefully regulated temperature for up to ten days, but four or five is usual. Through the fermentation, a head brewer takes gravity and pH readings to monitor the rate of fermentation. Once all of the sugars are fermented, the beer may be cooled to stabilize it. The yeast sediment is collected for re-use, and the wort is transferred to the conditioning tank.

▲ The brewer will always want to inspect the wort visually for clarity.

▼ Always keep an eye on the brewpot to avoid a boil-over during the hot break.

29

CONDITIONING

The temperature is kept at just above freezing in the aging tank. Excess yeast, proteins, and some tannins (a haze-forming compound) settle to the bottom of the tank over a period of time. Here the beer matures and mellows in flavor.

▶ At the end of the boil, a sample is drawn from the kettle for a specific-gravity reading.

▼ The final stage of the process—the beer is bottled and sent off to grocery stores, restaurants, and bars.

FILTERING

After conditioning, the beer may be filtered. The most common sort of filter is a plate-frame filter, a series of flat pads that trap tiny microorganisms from the beer.

THE HOLDING TANK

The filtered beer is kept in a vessel called the bright tank. Light carbon dioxide pressure may applied to the tank to carbonate the beer and keep it fresh as it awaits bottling, casking, or kegging.

HOMEBREWING

Brewer Scott Youmans made an interesting observation: "In microbrewing and homebrewing the big picture is the same. The difference between the two is that, while homebrewers tend to experiment with different recipes, we have to make the same beer batch after batch. So we have to fully understand the science behind brewing and make sure that the procedure is the same for every batch."

Homebrewers have the advantage of experimentation. Commercial breweries make batches for public sale. To stay in business, the brewery must produce quality beer that is consistent in color and taste.

As for consistency, well-informed homebrewers can control many aspects of the brewing process, and create beer to their specifications every time. As you read this book, you will learn how to predict how beer will turn out, and you will gain control over your procedure using Extract Homebrew Worksheets (see page 45).

BREWING YOUR FIRST BATCH OF BEER

The previous sections outlined the professional brewing process. Each aspect of homebrewing will be explored in greater detail in subsequent chapters, and advanced concepts and techniques will be introduced.

Nothing, however, whets the appetite for this type of learning more than making a tasty batch of homebrew. While the chemical processes that transpire in pot and fermenter are complex, the procedure can be relatively simple. The Sumerians made palatable potables without potholders—or even a stove—so fear not. By carefully following the instructions in this chapter, you'll produce an enjoyable, satisfying brew that would make even Ninkasi the beer goddess proud.

IN THIS CHAPTER YOU WILL LEARN:

All of the basic equipment and ingredients needed for your first batch
of homebrew
How to brew an extract-based recipe
How to fill out an Extract Homebrew Worksheet
Basic recipe variations and tips on how to improve your brew

INGREDIENTS

6³/₅ lb (3 kg) unhopped amber malt extract syrup or 5¹/₂ lb (2.5 kg) unhopped dry amber malt extract (dry extract is more concentrated than syrup, which is diluted in water, so less is needed)

1¹/₂ oz (40 g) Northern Brewer hop pellets (to provide your beer with a bitterness that will balance the sweetness of your malt)

1 oz (25 g) Cascade hop pellets (added at the end of the boil for hop flavor and aroma)

1056 Wyeast American ale yeast or one packet of dry ale yeast (The Wyeast is a liquid and comes in a "slap pack." Rupture an inner bladder with the palm of your hand, wait until the packet swells, usually in a day or two, and pour into your cooled wort)

5 oz (150g) corn sugar (used at bottling to carbonate your beer)

6 gallons (27 liters) tap water or bottled spring water. Expect to lose up to a gallon during the boil. The extra water ensures you'll have 5 gallons (23 liters) of beer in the fermenter

▲ Hops are a much-loved ingredient of beer.

EQUIPMENT

You may find that you already have some of this equipment lying around the kitchen and an hour of rummaging may save you some money. However, you probably won't find a hydrometer tucked away in your silverware drawer (unless you are obsessively concerned with the sugar content in your grape juice). For this and other items exclusive to homebrewing, you'll need to visit your local supply store.

Canning pot	3–6 gallon (14–27 liter) stainless-steel stockpot or enamelware canning pot. The larger the better and, for all practical purposes, stainless steel is best.
Smaller saucepan	This will be used for rehydrating dry yeast and liquefying priming sugar.
One or two long-handled stirring spoons	Wood can be used during the boil but sanitized plastic or stainless steel must be used when the wort is cool to avoid introduction of bacteria.
Cloth or muslin bags	Used to steep your hops, these are very cheap and very useful. Purchase three for your first batch.
Floating thermometer	This item, included in most kits, must be able to withstand boiling temperatures. You'll use it to gauge when your wort is cool enough for pitching (adding yeast), and to make hydrometer corrections.
Timer	Get one that counts backward.
Measuring cup	Make sure you use food-grade plastic.
Primary fermenter with lid and spigot	Food-grade plastic is good for beginners and the spigot makes transferring a breeze. There are two sizes available: 5 gallon and 6½ gallon (25 and 30 liter). You'll need the larger to ferment a 5-gallon (25-liter) batch.
Airlock and drilled rubber bung	Airlocks make high art of low tech. These small devices attach to your primary fermenter, allowing CO_2 to escape but keeping unwanted bacteria from gaining entrance. These are included in most kits.

Hydrometer	Usually included in basic kits, these are used to measure sugar content before and after fermentation to gauge attenuation and alcohol content.
Siphon hose	Food-grade, clear hose used to siphon beer from one container to another. This is included in most basic kits. If you buy it separately, make sure the inside diameter is $^3/_8$ in (0.9 cm) across.
Bottle filler	This hard plastic device connects to your siphon hose. Beer comes out only when the spring-activated tip is pressed into the bottom of your bottle. This is another simple but ingenious device that will save you volumes of otherwise spilled beer.
Bottle capper	There are hammer cappers, two-handed cappers, and bench cappers. The two-handed type is often included in basic kits and seems the best marriage of quality and price.
Bottle brush	Reaches into those hard-to-reach spaces and helps to remove those hard-to-remove spots.
52–54 brown "non-returnable" pop-top bottles	Light is the enemy of maturing beer, so stick with bottles that discourage its effects. Also, screw-top bottles are impossible to seal properly and are often too thin to withstand the pressures created by CO_2 during bottle conditioning. Often, your local watering hole will happily part with a few cases of empties for a couple of bucks.
52–54 bottle caps	These are available at your local supply store and are often included in basic kits.
Food-grade sanitizer	Used to sanitize your equipment. Your local homebrew shop will carry a number of sanitizing acids that can be diluted into a sanitizing solution. Note: Cleaning is different than sanitizing. You can't sanitize something that's dirty!

STEPS TO SUCCESSFUL BREWING

1. Cleaning and sanitizing your equipment and work area
2. Carefully following recipe procedure
3. Keeping thorough records

Sanitation is a must. The object is to minimize the amount of bacteria that come into contact with your wort, thus giving the yeast opportunity to ferment properly. Brewers who overlook this step are bound eventually to wind up with a batch of spoiled beer. Furthermore, they are sure to foster future bacterial infections if spotted, nicked, or gummy equipment is not promptly replaced or thoroughly cleaned and sanitized.

PREPARATION

Prepare at least a day in advance. If you are using a liquid yeast pack, rupture the inner bladder with your palm and knead its contents. The yeast needs a day or two to strengthen and multiply—the packet should inflate dramatically. Depending on your water source, you may want to dechlorinate your water by letting it sit in your open fermenter overnight or by adding Campden tablets. Any water allowed prolonged exposure to air must be boiled. Most of this goes in your brewpot, so it is no problem.

Water reserved for addition into the fermenter should be boiled in a open pot and cooled in a covered container or drawn straight from the faucet or bottle. Alternatively, boil your water for 10 minutes before adding extract. A boil drives off most of the chlorine, and will clear "hard" water of some minerals. Next, pour most of the boiling water into another vessel and rinse your brewpot. Now pour your water back into the pot and add your malt.

Sanitize your equipment using food grade sanitizer. Different sanitizers require different contact times to be effective, so be sure to read instructions carefully. Dirty equipment should be cleaned using hot water and a little detergent, but rinse thoroughly, as any soap residue will discourage the head retention of your beer and can potentially leave undesirable flavors. When cleaning equipment, avoid stiff brushes and abrasive scrubbing tools. These scuff plastic items, creating tiny cavities where nasty microbes can live. Once your equipment is cleaned and sanitized, rinse with water that has been boiled for a few minutes. Keep your sanitized equipment in a clean environment. You can use your fermenting bucket to contain smaller items, but again, take care not to damage its interior.

Next clean your work area. Scrub your counters and stovetop and sweep and mop the floor. A final once-over with a sponge soaked in the sanitizing solution will ensure that kitchen bugs are wiped away. You can minimize airborne contaminants by filling a spray bottle with sanitizing solution or isopropyl alcohol and misting the area. However, make sure all of your ingredients are safely tucked away.

◀ Most brewing supply stores sell a starter kit for the novice homebrewer.

BREWING

Now, lay all of your ingredients out. If you're using canned malt extract syrup, you may want to place the cans in hot water to make the contents easier to pour. I don't recommend boiling them in a pot of water on the stove, as the heat can scorch the syrup. This will change the color of your beer, and negatively affect its flavor. Rather, fill a basin with near-boiling water, crimp a hole in each can with a can-opener, and ease them in. Ten minutes should be plenty of time.

Fill your brewpot to three-quarters full of water. Bring this to a boil, then remove the pot from the heat. Stir in your extract. Pour some hot water into the can to remove all of the extract. (Be careful not to burn your hands!) Stir until certain that all of it has dissolved. Undissolved extract will sink to the bottom, scorching when you reapply heat to the brewpot.

Now place 1 oz (28 g) Northern Brewer hops into a hop bag and tie a knot in the top. Return your uncovered brewpot to the heat and continue to stir. As the wort approaches boiling, a foamy surface will form. This is called the hot break. If the foam starts to rise, turn down the heat or spray in clean water. The hot break can last from 5 to 15 minutes, so watch until the milky surface dissolves into a boil.

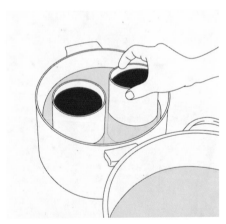

1. *Place the extract in hot water.*

2. *Add the extract to the brewpot.*

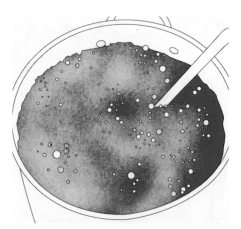

3. *Keep an eye on the brewpot! Use a mist bottle or adjust the temperature on your range to avoid a boil-over during the hot break.*

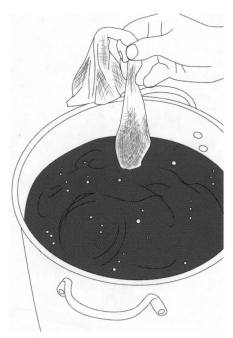

4. *Add the boiling hops.*

Drop the hop bag into the pot and start your timer at 60 minutes. Stir and watch the pot, as adding hops can cause it to rise again. If this happens, adjust the heat or spray clean water into the pot. At the 30-minute mark, drop in the other ½ oz (14 g) Northern Brewer hops in the same manner as the first addition. At the 5-minute mark, add the Cascade hops in a muslin bag.

After 60 minutes, cover the brewpot and transfer it to a basin filled with ice water. Begin your timer. Remove hops bags using a sanitized spoon, taking care to avoid splashing. Your goal is to bring the wort from near-boiling down to about 75°F (24°C) as quickly as possible; wort is susceptible to bacteria within the range 80–140°F (27–60°C). It is now ready for the fermenter.

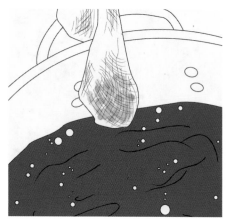

5. *Add your finishing hops 5 minutes before the end of the boil.*

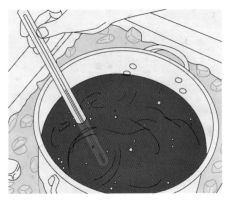

6. *Cool the wort as quickly as possible.*

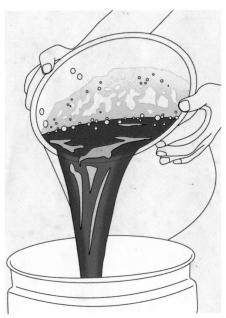

7. *Pour the cooled wort into your primary fermenter.*

Fill your fermenter with about ½ gallon (2 liters) of cold, clean water. Pour the contents of the brewpot into the fermenter. This is the only time that oxidation is not a concern. In fact, the introduction of oxygen is vital at this point, since the yeast will need it during the first (aerobic) stage of fermentation. Topping off your fermenter to the 5-gallon (25-liter) mark with preboiled, cold water should bring your wort to pitching temperature (74–78°F/23–26°C). Take a temperature reading, and place the lid on loosely. Draw a small amount of wort from the spigot on the fermenter and take a hydrometer reading. Be sure to spin your hydrometer in the vial to clear away bubbles. Take the reading from the top of the meniscus

(the highest level of the curved surface). If the wort temperature is above 60°F (16°C)—and it probably will be—use a hydrometer correction table for an accurate reading. It should be at or around 1.056. If it isn't, don't worry; different brands of extract will often supply varying amounts of sugars and carbohydrates. This is your original gravity.

Pitch the yeast. If using liquid, simply snip a corner of the packet with sanitized scissors and stir in the contents. For dry yeast, rehydrate in preboiled, warm (90°F/32°C) water or distilled water and cover with plastic wrap for 10 minutes. Pour contents into the fermenter and stir. In both cases continue to stir wort for 5–10 minutes, encouraging oxygen.

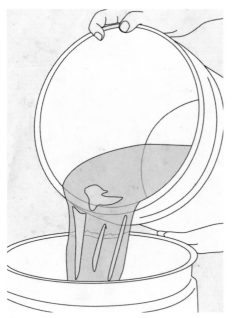

8. *Top the fermenter off to the 5-gallon (25-liter) mark with cold, clean water.*

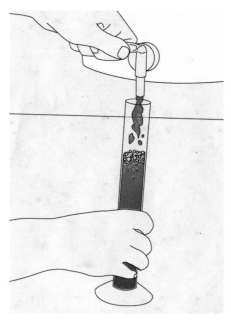

9. *Draw off a sample into your hydrometer vial.*

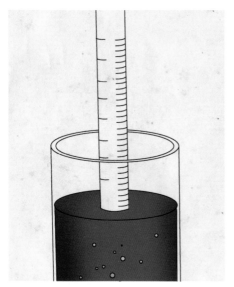

10. *Make sure you spin your hydrometer to clear away surface bubbles. This is your original gravity reading. Drink it!*

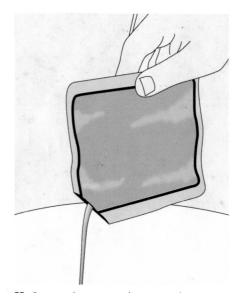

11. *Pour in the prepared yeast packet.*

Fill your sanitized airlock with water or high-proof vodka and wedge it into the hole on the lid of the fermenting bucket. Store your fermenter in a dark, quiet place, and clean your equipment.

Ideally, you should notice bubbles plopping up through your airlock in less than 24 hours. This is good. A short lag time—the time taken for the bubbling to start—is the start of healthy fermentation. It means that the yeast has eaten the oxygen and entered the anaerobic, alcohol- and CO_2-producing stage. This may last 4 days to a week. When the bubbling has stopped, wait 2 more days, check the final gravity of the beer (yes, it's beer now), and get ready to bottle it.

Use your bottle brush and warm water from the faucet to wash each bottle. Make sure any spotty or gooey deposits are completely gone. Soak clean bottles in a solution of sanitizer. Rinse each bottle with preboiled, warm water, or allow it to air-dry. Immerse your bottle caps in a sanitizing solution for 20 minutes. Never boil the caps, since heat will ruin the rubber seals. Sanitize and rinse your siphon hose and bottle filler.

Now add 5 oz (150 g) corn sugar into about a cup (225 ml) of water and stir to a boil. After 5 minutes, remove the pot from the heat. Draw some beer out of the fermenter for a final-gravity reading. Your hydrometer should read about 1.014. Again, if you are off by a few points, don't sweat it.

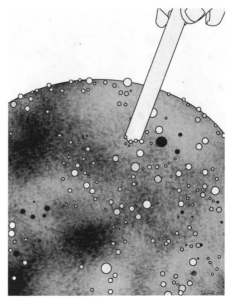

12. *Stir the wort with a sanitized spoon to encourage the introduction of oxygen.*

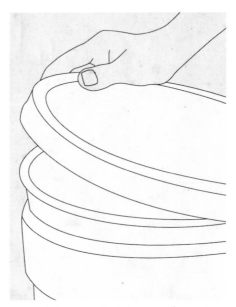

13. *Tightly secure the lid on your fermenter.*

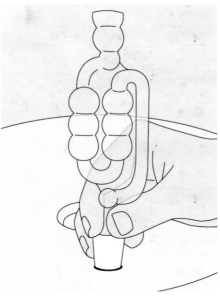

14. *Fill your airlock with water or vodka and wedge it in the hole of the lid of your bucket.*

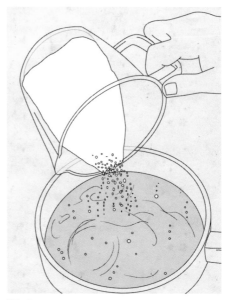

15. *Pour your corn sugar into a saucepan partially filled with water. Bring the mixture to a boil.*

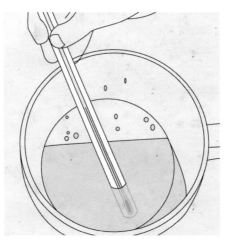

16. *When the mixture has cooled, you can add it to your fermenter.*

17. *Pour the priming sugar into your fermenter and gently mix, taking care not to disturb any sediment on the bottom of the bucket.*

Remove the fermenter lid and, with a sanitized spoon, gently stir in the corn mixture. This added sugar will give your yeast a "boost in the bottle," carbonating your beer.

Attach the siphon hose to the fermenter spigot and the bottle filler to the siphon hose. Gather your bottles together, get out your caps and capper. It's time to bottle!

Turn on the spigot. Place the tip of the bottle filler in one of the bottles and press. When the beer is almost level with the bottle rim, remove the filler. This gives you the ³/₄ in (2 cm) space for carbonation. Any more and you'll end up with flat beer, and less will cause a gaseous buildup meaning your bottle could explode! Place a cap over the bottle and proceed until all bottles are filled. Crimp each bottle, mark the crown with a distinguishing mark, (e.g. #1 for first beer brewed), and rinse them. Store for 2 weeks in a warm, dark place—around 68°F (20°C) is ideal. Bottling and kegging are explored in detail later.

After 2 weeks, cool a bottle and pop the cap. You should hear a hiss, the sound of excess CO_2 escaping. The sediment at the bottom of each bottle is normal and mainly composed of flocculated yeast cells, some protein and hop material. Sediment is rich in vitamin B12, but will make your beer taste extra-yeasty—leave it in the bottle. Enjoy!

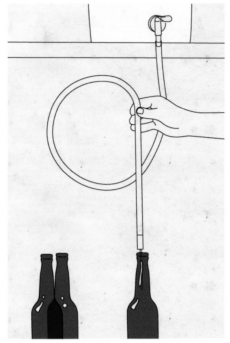

18. *Line your bottles up and get ready to fill!*

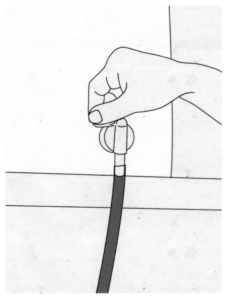

19. *Turn the spigot on.*

20. *Place the bottle filler in a bottle, press to fill, and pull it out when the beer is near the rim.*

21. *Crimp each bottle and mark as "First Batch."*

EXTRACT HOMEBREW WORKSHEETS

Make your own Extract Homebrew Worksheets, which are designed to condense essential procedural information into a single, accessible page. Include space for data such as equipment and ingredients used, procedural information, notes, and a results section. If you want to perfect a particular style, or are simply experimenting with ideas, you'll have a "journal" that can be referenced and expanded.

These kind of worksheets allow any extract-based recipe to be entered. Divide each worksheet into three sections: Homebrew Recipe, Equipment/Ingredient Checklist & Procedural Schedule, and Post-boil Procedures & Results (see pages 46–47).

The first two sections will be filled out before you brew. In the Homebrew

Recipe section, you are simply entering the recipe you are following. For the recipe that follows, for example, just enter the ingredients.

▲ Keep thorough records to replicate a good batch and identify and correct mistakes.

HOMEBREW RECIPE

This section allows you to create an equipment roster and itemize your ingredients according to when each is added. Note that ingredient times are entered according to the total time of boil. This type of scheduling is easy—you "check off" each addition when the correct time is reached—and it will allow you greater control over the procedure as you learn more about the craft.

INGREDIENTS

6½ lb (3 kg) Amber unhopped extract syrup
1½ oz (40 g) Northern Brewer hops
1 oz (25 g) Cascade hops
1 packet Wyeast American ale yeast
5 oz (150 g) corn sugar
6 gallons (27 liters) tap water

Equipment	Ingredients	Time(s) Added
1. 5-gallon (25-liter) stainless steel pot	6½ lb (3 kg) extract syrup	At beginning of boil
2. Plastic spoon		
3. Floating thermometer		
4. Fermenting bucket		
5. Hydrometer	1 oz (25 g) Northern Brewer hops	At 60 minutes
6. Timer	½ oz (12 g) Northern Brewer hops	At 30 minutes
7. Siphon hose	1 oz (25 g) Cascade hops	At 5 minutes
8. Bottle filler		
9. 52 x 12-oz (350-g) brown bottles	Notes	Notes
10. 52 bottle caps		
11. 2 new spray bottles		
12. 3 muslin hop bags		
13. Measuring cup		

The final section will be completed as each phase of the process is performed.

EQUIPMENT/INGREDIENT CHECKLIST
& PROCEDURAL SCHEDULE
POST-BOIL PROCEDURES & RESULTS

Fermentation	Bottling	Results
OG: 1.056	Date Bottled: 2/4	
Pitching Temp: 72ºF (22ºC)	Date of 1st tasting: 2/11	First beer tasted good! I'll go against my urges and wait another week before trying the next one.
Cooling time: 35 mins	Date of 2nd tasting: 2/19	Second beer is excellent! Well-balanced bitterness, and the cascade hops produce a great aroma and lingering flavor! I like the color, but there is some cloudiness. I'll see what I can do to clear this great beer up!
Started fermenting: 1/25		
Racked? Y/N Days:		
Ceased fermenting: 2/1		
FG: 1.016		

◀▲ These simple worksheet outlines will help you learn how to homebrew more quickly and efficiently. As your knowledge and experience increase, so too will the quality of your brew!

VARIATIONS ON A THEME

EXPERIMENTING WITH THE BASIC RECIPE

Now that you've brewed your first batch, you know the basics of homebrewing. View this knowledge as the basic notes of a complex musical composition. Soon, you'll be orchestrating malt, water, hops, and yeast with the finesse of a great conductor. For now, you can "riff" off your basic knowledge, changing ingredients and procedure to create several variations of the basic recipe, while gaining experience through practice.

AGING IN A SECONDARY FERMENTER

You can further age and clarify your homebrew by using a secondary vessel. This allows you to transfer your fermented beer off the sedimented material and yeast, and store your beer without fear of contamination or off flavors from the trub.

The best container is a 5-gallon (25-liter) glass carboy. These are used commercially to store chemicals and drinking water, though the latter is quickly being replaced with plastic. You can find carboys at your local homebrew supplier or, if you're lucky, at flea markets and garage sales. You'll also need a rubber stopper that fits the mouth of the carboy (no, the one you use for your plastic fermernter won't fit), and an airlock.

Once primary fermentation is complete, sanitize a length of transfer tubing. Place your primary (plastic bucket) fermenter on a table. Sanitize the carboy and place it on the floor, under the bucket. Attach the transfer tube to the spigot on your primary fermenter. Place the other end of the tubing in the carboy, so that it reaches all the way to the bottom. You don't want any splashing at this point, because the introduction of air will hasten oxidation. Open the valve on the spigot and gently begin to siphon. Transfer the liquid until the level in the bucket reaches the level of the spigot. Now remove the hose, attach the airlock, and store your conditioning beer in a dark, cool area.

You can also use a carboy as a primary fermenter. Many homebrewers prefer these because they are less prone to scratches and scuffs, which can harbor bacteria.

Doubtless, there will be times when you want quick ale. In this case you can bottle once primary fermentation has ceased. However, there are many benefits to racking your brew. Racking to a secondary fermenter allows your beer to mature, to mellow in flavor, or gain flavor from the addition of fruits or hops. A couple of weeks in a secondary fermenter allows your beer to settle. With or without the addition of clarifying agents, your homebrew will have more sparkle and less murk. Finally, beer that has been transferred off fermentation sediment can be stored for long periods of time, and bottled or kegged at your leisure.

You can greatly hasten the sedimentation of yeast and many other matter by "crash-cooling" your brew just after primary fermentation. Transfer your fermented beer into a secondary vessel and refrigerate (about 34°F/1°C) for several days. This works especially well for beers that are going to be artificially carbonated in a keg, since much of the suspended yeast is dropped out of solution. Still, there should be enough yeast

▲ A swing-top or "Emily" capper is one of the most cost-effective and easy to use bottle cappers available.

floating around for bottle conditioning. It may just take a bit longer. Crash-cooling subdues yeasty flavors in beer that matures at higher temperatures.

Another way to aid in yeast sedimentation is the use of fining agents. The addition of gelatin or isinglass in the secondary fermenter will help yeast drop to the bottom of the vessel so the clear beer can be siphoned off the sediment.

CHAPTER 2

INGREDIENTS

A musical quartet has only four instruments, but in the right hands those instruments can come together to produce a nearly infinite range of musical expression. Beer, at its most basic, contains four ingredients: malt, hops, yeast, and water. Yet those same humble ingredients can be commanded to create everything from a straw-colored bitter that looks like sunshine in a glass, to a wheat whose swirling flavors dance on the tongue, to an opaque stout that pours like midnight and warms the belly on a crisp autumn day.

The following sections explore the ingredients used by homebrewers in greater detail. We will cover the four essential ingredients, as well as adjuncts and other additions that push the possibilities even further. Also included in these sections are tips on how to use and store each ingredient.

By understanding how each ingredient affects the characteristics of your homebrew, you will gain knowledge of and control over the procedure. The end result is better beer and more consistent results.

MALT

▲ Barley is one of the earliest recorded cereals to be used for making beer.

From the beginning, malt has been the major ingredient in beer. Malt influences color, body, and flavor. The reddish glow of an English pale ale and the silky darkness of a stout are determined by malt. Likewise, the crisp body of a weizen and the heavy sweetness of a barley wine are each largely due to the type and amount of malt used. Malt provides fuel for the yeast and is the sweet polar partner to the bitter hop.

BARLEY BASICS

Known to botanists as *Hordeum vulgare*, barley belongs to the grass family. The use of barley in the making of bread and beer dates back about 10,000 years. It is singular in its ability to thrive in extreme climates, and is one of the most abundant crops—wild and cultivated. Though wheat has supplanted barley for breadmaking, barley is still used for cereals, animal feed, and, of course, beer.

Two major types of barley that are used in brewing are the six- and two-row varieties. Six-row barley has more fertile kernels per ear than the two-row type. However, the kernels on the latter are larger and more consistently sized. Two-row barley is more commonly used as the primary grist (main malt base) in homebrewing with six-row sometimes added to supply certain other qualities.

Each kernel of barley is a seed. Like any seed it has all of the basic components needed for such a task. There is a protective covering (the husk), an internal food source (the starchy endosperm), and the infant germ itself (the embryo).

As rain is absorbed up through the plant, the kernels become heavy. The moisture-laden kernels break from their connecting axis and fall to the soil. Enzymes within each kernel are released, breaking down starches into usable sugars. Soon the feeding embryo within the grain sprouts rootlets and an acrospires, rooting itself into the ground. This natural process is called germination.

THE MALTING PROCESS

The malting process is controlled germination. Maltsters replicate natural phenomena by steeping and germination, and then dry the kernels in a kiln. This procedure ensures a good portion of the endosperm becomes fermentable compounds, but that the conversion is left incomplete. When the germination process is stopped dictates the degree to which the barley is "modified"— that is, to what degree the long-chain molecules are broken down. Well-modified malt contains enzyme-degradable materials that give body, sweetness, and alcohol to beer.

Steeping the grains takes place in a water-filled vat. The water is changed regularly to discourage microbial contamination, and one or more "air-rests" ensure that the kernels don't die from lack of oxygen. During this time, barley absorbs water. When the moisture content of the kernels is about 150 percent, they are germinated.

Here, the kernels are spread out and held at 60°F (16°C) for about 4 to 6 days. During this time, air is blown onto the kernels to promote aerobic respiration—replicating what happens

▲ Malted barley gives beer its characteristic flavor and all of its color.

in the wild. The grains are turned to keep sprouting shoots from becoming entangled, and to discourage decay. It is here that the hard endosperm is attacked by starch-degrading enzymes within the grain, creating shorter-chain starches and sugars. Once the acrospire reaches a length of about three-quarters that of the kernel, the grains are dried. This modified barley is termed "green malt."

Kilning the grains is a delicately controlled drying process that slowly raises the temperature of the grains to about 120–30°F (49–54°C) over 30 to 35 hours. This slow increase in heat preserves enzymes needed later, and keeps the husks pale.

At this point the malt is ready to be used in brewing. Further heating is necessary to produce "specialty malts"—malts that add flavor or color but cannot form the bulk of fermentable materials.

MALT FORMS AND CHARACTERISTICS

There are three basic forms of malt. Malt extract is malt that has been mashed in a kettle and concentrated into either a syrup or powder. Specialty malts are malts that have been further treated in the kiln to darken the color and create various flavors. This extra roasting and toasting often destroys enzymes within the kernel necessary to convert starches to sugar during the mash. Therefore, these malts are used in small amounts, along with extracts or other grains, to enhance the flavor, color, body, and head-retention of beer. Brewing malts can be used for the bulk of the grist. Professional and all-grain brewers use malt grain for the same reason as extract brewers use concentrates. However, unlike extracts, malt grains must first be mashed to convert starches in the endosperm into fermentable sugars. Both specialty and brewing malts are introduced into the wort

▼ A barrel of barley kernels—they undergo a drying process before brewing.

or water as grains. While their respective protective husks influence color, most of the desirable material lies within. Therefore, grains must be gently cracked prior to use, to make the modified kernels accessible to the brew liquor. Just how and to what degree these grains should be cracked will be explored later.

Since your progression from novice to intermediate will follow a path of incremental steps toward more complex procedures, we'll take a closer look at each form in the order that you'll likely be using them.

MALT EXTRACT

Malt extract is the product of professionally mashed wort that has been concentrated into either dry or syrup form. In the past the extract brewer was limited by a scarcity of quality products. Today, demand has prompted the emergence of a spectrum of extracts, covering almost every conceivable style. There are light, pale, amber, dark, and wheat malt extracts available in either hopped or unhopped forms. When buying any of the above, try to avoid the prehopped extracts. Even as a novice you should have the freedom to determine which style of hops you want to pair with your extract, and you'll have more control over the flavor of your finished brew.

Extract syrup is composed of about 20 percent water, so is not quite as concentrated as dry extract. Therefore, for a recipe calling for 1 lb (500 g) of liquid extract, use an 80 percent conversion factor when making substitutions, so 1 lb XME = 1.2 lb LME and 1 lb LME = 0.8 lb DME.

Many homebrewers use extract as their primary source of malt in their brew because many men and women find

▲ Malted and raw grains are roasted at a high temperature to create a specialty malt.

that investing the 2 hours it takes to make beer using extracts beats spending all day in the garage mashing and lautering. This is not to say that extract brewing is simple. Many very bad beers have been made using extract syrup. The difference between the all-grain brewer and the extract brewer is that the latter has much more control over the composition of the extract. Once the all-grain brewer is finished sparging, he or she is at the point that the extract brewer is when the syrup is stirred into the brewpot. From that point on, the two are on equal footing.

▲ Pale malt, crystal malt, chocolate malt, wheat malt, and aromatic hops.

SPECIALTY MALT

The addition of specialty malt will greatly enhance the quality and variety of your homebrew. With just a few extra steps and a couple of pieces of equipment, you'll produce homebrew that is fresher-tasting, fuller-bodied, and more accurately tailored to you.

Crystal malt Sometimes called caramel malt, this is used to enhance sweetness, body, and color. Crystal malt is made by kilning undried green malt to mashing temperatures (150–158°F/66–70°C). This converts the starches into sugar. The malt is then kilned at higher temperatures, "crystallizing" the interior sugars into a hard glassy mass. Further kilning dictates the final color of the malt, which ranges from a light, strawlike color to a deep caramel.

Chocolate malt Used in darker beers, this is dried malt that has been roasted in a kiln until a dark-brown color is reached. Higher temperatures produce the chocolate color, but care is taken to maintain a smooth, uncharred flavor.

Black patent malt Ever notice the sharp, espresso-like flavor of a dry stout? Then you have most likely tasted the effects of this very high-kilned malt.

Dextrin or Carapils® malt This light malt contributes little flavor to beer, but is used to enhance body and promote head retention.

Victory malt This British malt lends a toasted flavor to dark lagers and ales. Used often in brown ale and porter, the aroma is perceived as biscuit-like.

USING SPECIALTY GRAINS

The addition of specialty malt is a simple procedure. If you are using an electric range, simply add the cracked grains via a cloth or nylon grain bag (available at most supply stores) to 3–5 gallons (14–23 liters) of cold water. Heat the water to near boiling and scoop out the bag with tongs or a fork, then squeeze the liquid back into the pot without using your hands. You can drape the bag over the pot and use your spoon to extract the "goodness," or use two kitchen plates held over the pot and squeezed like a vise. Bring your water to a boil and proceed as if you were making an extract brew. For more control, and possibly a better yield, heat your water to a temperature of about 155°F (68°C).

Next, remove the grain bag and extract the liquid as described above. This method makes better use of the grains, and also protects against tannic (dry, astringent) off flavors derived from grain husk.

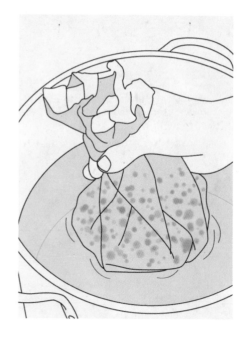

1. Heat the water to 155ºF (68ºC).

2. Put the grains into the water and steep for 30-45 minutes. Using a straining bag allows for "no mess" grain additions.

Continues overleaf...

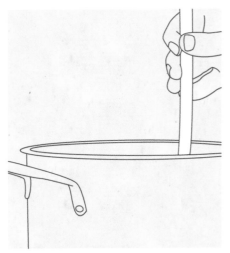

3. *Gently stir to aid in the extraction of "goodness" from the grains.*

4. *Maintain a temperature of 150–158ºF (66–70ºC).*

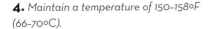

MALT TIPS

- Avoid prehopped extract.
- Store unused DME in a sealed container away from heat and moisture.
- Store unused grains in an airtight plastic container.
- Malt syrup contains about 20 percent water. If substituting DME, use 20 percent less of the powder.
- Never boil grains, because material in the husk will negatively affect your homebrew.
- Find and use only fresh, good-quality malts and malt extracts.

GRAIN MALT

Brewer's malt, or simply malt, is often used as the primary grist by professional breweries. Unlike specialty malts, these contain enzymes that convert starches into sugars during the mash. The quantity of enzymes in malt is referred to as diastase—a lot of starch-converting enzymes means high diastatic power. This means that it contains a high degree of alpha amylase and beta amylase—which will degrade chains of glucose into shorter chains in the mash.

While all-grain brewers use malt as the whole grist, the extract brewer can use these malts to enhance the flavor, color, and body of his or her beer. This relatively simple step will give you more control over your process, raising you to the level: intermediate brewer.

Pale malt comes in several varieties. Six-row brewer's malt contains a higher level of starch-degrading enzymes than its two-row

◀▼ Palm is a Belgian beer brand that specializes in creating a wholesome, malty aroma.

counterpart, but less sugar. The kernels are relatively small, so the grain husk comprises a high percentage of the total malt. Since too much husk material will contribute undesirable characteristics (such as haze and astringency), six-row malt is rarely used as the predominant source of grist. Two-row brewer's malt has more viable starch per husk, but has fewer enzymes to convert the starch. In some cases, a small quantity of six-row malt is added to larger amounts of two-row to boost diastatic power. However, modern two-row malts can produce fully attenuated brews without additional enzymes. An example of a common malt used in partial-mash brewing is wheat malt. This is used primarily in German and Belgian ales. Often used with special yeast cultures, this light malt combined with malted barley produces light, thirst-quenching beers.

HOPS

Nearly 6,000 years of brewing coasted along hops-free, before brewers discovered that the bitter flowers on the plant provided a pleasing balance to the sweetness of the malt.

Historians believe people started brewing with hops in the late 800s CE. Originally, they were probably added for flavor, although it wasn't long before brewers began to notice that hops also helped stabilize and preserve beer. By the sixteenth century, the use of hops had spread throughout Europe. In 1516, Bavaria enacted the Reinheitsgebot, a purity law that constrained German brewers to the use of only three ingredients: barley, water, and hops.

For a time, the English regarded hops with suspicion, and Henry VIII even tried to ban the import of any hopped beer. Still, like the hardy profuseness of the plant itself, the superior qualities of this once "noxious weed" were, eventually proclaimed as self-evident.

Today hops are prized for the wide range of characteristics they add to beer. Certain plants are cultivated for use as bittering agents, others for aroma and flavor. Brewers label the two major groups as boiling or

▼ Fresh hops—the biggest hop-producing region is the Yakima Valley, in Oregon.

bittering hops, and finishing or aromatic hops, respectively. Many hop varieties include qualities of bitterness, flavor, and aroma, so I'll use the term boiling hops for hops added to the brewpot for 30 minutes or more, and finishing hops for those added at the end of the boil or later. To understand the differences between these two groups, let's discuss this wondrously versatile plant.

CULTIVATION AND ANATOMY

This tenacious bine is dioecious, which means there are both male and female varieties,

▼ Dried hops—they are used at different times for bittering or adding aroma and flavor.

though only the female is used in brewing. Hops are of the same family as the hemp plant and, like their infamous cousin, produce dense, conelike flowers. Hops are usually planted in March or April and harvested the first week of September. While this perennial plant produces buds throughout the summer, a mature bine will offer the most valuable yields at the season's end. Once harvested, the flowers are dried and packaged.

Each flower, or strobile, is composed of leaflike petals called bracteole. Bracteole produce lupulin, which appear as a fine yellow powder at the base of the petal. Actually, these are tiny glands that contain the resins and oils that contribute all the desired characteristics to beer. Resins give beer bitterness, while oils impart a range of flavor and bouquet. Since high levels of the bitter resin will dominate the gentler notes afforded by the oils, the two groups are roughly differentiated by the amount of resin in the plant.

BITTER RESINS

Lupulin glands contain two major resins: alpha acid and beta acid. Beta acid is almost completely insoluble at normal wort pH levels, and contributes little flavor to the finished beer. Your main concern is with the alpha acid. Herein lies all the potential bitterness needed for a well-balanced homebrew. Unlike beta acids, alphas become soluble in solution with the addition of heat. This process, called isomerization, allows the wort to retain the bittering qualities from the resins. A minimum of 20 minutes at full boil is necessary to catalyze the resins into usable form. So-called iso-alpha acids remain in suspension throughout fermentation, storage, and, most importantly, in your glass, though they do degrade with time. Hoppy beer is always better fresh.

AA AND AAU

If you want to calculate how much potential bitterness a particular type of hops could give your beer, you need to know how much alpha acid the plant contains. Any respectable supplier of hops will list the percentage of alpha acids (AA percent) on the package. The range runs from around 3 percent (mild) to 20 percent (bitter!). Alpha Acid Units (AAU) use the alpha acid percentage of a particular hop multiplied by its weight in ounces, to calculate bittering potential. The author and homebrewer David Line devised this formula:

AA percent x weight (oz)
of hops used = AAU

Most extract-based recipes list the style and quantity of hops required. If, however, you don't have access to the listed hop, you can substitute a variety with a similar alpha-acid percentage.

If your supplier has neither the right hops nor a substitute that matches the alpha percentage you require, you can use AAUs to substitute. For example, if a recipe calls for 2 oz (50 g) of 7.5 percent Northern Brewer hops, the AAUs would be:

7.5 percent x 2 oz (50 g) = 15 AAU

This means 2 oz (50 g) Northern Brewer hops gives your beer 15 AAUs. Now, say you are using Brewers Gold hops, with an alpha acid content of 8.5 percent. How many ounces do you use to produce the same bitterness potential (15 AAUs)? Reverse the formula:

$$\frac{15 \text{ AAUs}}{8.5 \text{ AA percent}} = 1\frac{3}{4} \text{ oz (49 g)}$$

◀ Hops waiting to be harvested in the Willamette Valley of Oregon, one of the top hop-producing regions in the world.

however, have the luxury of experimental indulgence. We can toss an extra ounce or two of hops in the kettle on a whim, because in the bitter end we have no one to please but ourselves.

Keep in mind that AAUs predict bittering potential, not actual yield. Several factors determine how much iso-alpha acid makes its way into your glass. High-gravity beers, for example, require more hops to achieve the same balance as lighter-bodied beers. Other variants include hop form (whole, pellet, etc.), freshness, and when the hops are added to the wort. Many recipes call for bittering hops to be added in a couple of stages. This allows the wort to retain a maximum yield, by not becoming oversaturated with too much hops at once. Also, not all hops are the same. Different varieties will impart a wide range of flavors and aromas.

So how can you predict how bitter your final brew will taste? The quick answer is to say that you can't, exactly. Brewers use International Bitterness Units (IBU) as a measure of the actual bitterness in beer. 1 IBU = one part per million of isomerized alpha acid. All of the major styles of beer have IBU ranges, required to accurately represent their respective characteristics.

Several ingenious people have devised formulas to help predict IBUs—many are simple, some are staggeringly complex. In the Intermediate Brewing chapter (pages 116–147) you'll be introduced to one method you may find useful. In the meantime, don't worry about it. Even the most sophisticated predictive methods fail to consistently foretell actual bitterness. For now, just have fun experimenting. Professional breweries achieve consistency by controlled settings, repetition, and by blending several batches until a standard is met. We homebrewers don't have the equipment and time to do this. We do,

HOP TIPS

- Always make sure your hops are fresh.
- If you buy hops packaged in clear plastic, make sure the lupulin powder is yellow.
- Avoid rusty or brown-colored hops; it means the hops are oxidized and worthless.
- If you plan on storing hops, seal them in two airtight bags and keep them in your freezer.
- Add boiling hops in stages during the boil to ensure maximum bittering yield.
- Use cloth or muslin bags for a cheap, efficient way to add and remove hops.
- Avoid oxidation and "skunky" aromas by keeping your hops and fermenting wort away from sunlight.
- If you're dry-hopping with plug or whole hops, try dropping a few sanitized marbles into the hop bag, for sinking weight. This will give your hops maximum exposure to the brew.

AROMATIC OILS

The other qualities hops give to beer are flavor and aroma. For example, the distinctive spicy finish of a Pilsner Urquell is due, in part, to the oils found within the Saaz hop. While boiling hops balance homebrew, finishing hops crown the brew with smells and tastes that please the nose and linger on the palate. Terms like "citrusy," "floral," and "fruity" describe the delicate virtues proffered by these hops.

Like the flavor they impart, oils are much gentler than resins and will be destroyed by an extended boil. Therefore, finishing hops are best added to the wort in the final few minutes of the boil.

Another method for adding these hops is dry hopping. This involves adding the finishing hops during the second stage of fermentation or, if you have the equipment, directly into the keg along with the finished beer. This process gives beer a fresher aroma and flavor than finishing hops that are boiled. As a novice, you may be using a single-fermentation system. If this is the case, forget about dry hopping for now. Adding hops to the primary fermenter is not an effective way of imparting hop character. Much of the aroma may be scrubbed away by the CO_2 released during fermentation, or trapped in the trub by dead yeast cells. Hops can be added to a secondary fermenter, when the yeast activity has slowed somewhat.

If you are at a point where you are maturing your brew in a secondary fermenter, here is a simple method. Sanitize a small muslin bag by boiling it for about 20 minutes. With clean (but not soapy!) hands, put the hops in the bag and tie it off at the top. After you drop in the bag, close the fermenter and leave it alone. Since they are relatively high in acids, fresh hops have an antiseptic quality that heavily discourages the growth of bacteria, so adding hops to maturing beer

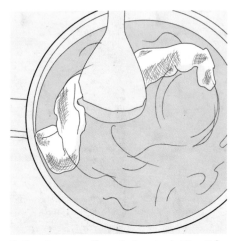

1. *Sanitize a small muslin bag by boiling it for about 20 minutes.*

2. *Put the hops in the bag, tie off the top, and drop the bag into the secondary fermenter.*

3. *Once you have dropped the bag into the fermenter, close it and leave it alone!*

will do no harm so long as you've followed good cleaning and sanitation procedures.

All hops are unique in their own way, and each will give your beer a slightly different flavor and bouquet. Alone, this can be magnificent. Working in concert, they are pure magic.

FORMS AND STORAGE

Hops are available in many forms. The two most common and practical are plug hops and hop pellets. Plug hops are whole hops that have been compressed into about a ½-in (1-cm) by 1-in (2.5-cm) disk. Hop pellets are machine-pulverized whole hops, formed into tiny pellets. Both of these forms have advantages over using whole hops. For one, more varieties of pelletized hops are available to homebrewers than whole hops. And it's easier to store a few ounces, double-bagged in your freezer, than trying to cram a bushel or two of whole hops alongside your frozen yogurt.

That said, whole hops do have a valuable role in homebrewing. While it may be impractical to use them as your entire source of hops, whole hops are regarded highly for their aromatic and flavoring qualities. Some argue that pellets dilute or alter the chemical composition of the oils or lend a more grassy flavor. Whole hops contain lupulin glands that are totally intact. This is still under debate, so you should feel free to experiment.

Whichever form you choose, it is essential that you store hops away from warmth and air. Hops left on the counter will begin to oxidize in as little time as a week. Fresh hops give your homebrew distinct character. Stale, oxidized hops have less to offer and can negatively affect the flavor of your beer. Store unused hops inside two well-sealed plastic bags in the freezer.

▲ Roasted barley and dried hops formed into pellets for ease of use.

YEAST

If malt provides the fuel needed to transform wort into beer, then yeast is the engine powering the process.

Yeast consumes malt sugars, and transforms them into roughly equal parts of alcohol and carbon dioxide through a process called fermentation. Yet yeast does much more than this. Brewers count on yeast to metabolize malt sugars into alcohol. However, like the reaction that happens in the car engine, yeast produces a number of by-products. Luckily, many of these are desirable, and even define certain styles of beer. Others are less desirable, and care must be taken to minimize their effects. Different strains of yeast produce varying degrees of by-product, and this will be explored in greater detail later.

YEAST TIPS

- Buy only fresh yeast that is properly packaged and stored in a refrigerator.
- Thoroughly aerate your cool wort before adding yeast.
- Always maintain sanitary conditions when preparing or pitching yeast.
- Store your fermenter in a dark place at temperatures consistent with the recommended range.
- Primary-ferment lagers at temperatures between 65-70ºF (18-21ºC). Rack to a secondary and slowly lower the temperature to 34-48ºF (1-9ºC).
- Pitch enough yeast to assure a fast and healthy fermentation.

WILD AND CRAZY GUYS

Yeast is a single-celled fungus. Thousands of species exist, adapted to almost every climate. Most species are wild, and too mutable to be relied on for the purposes of brewing. As single-celled species, they can evolve within a few generations, depending on changing hosts and environments. Thanks to men like Louis Pasteur and Jacob Christian Jacobson, understanding these fungal fermenters has led to the cultivation of the reliable yeast strains we use to this day.

THE TAMING OF THE BREW

The major strains of yeast available to the homebrewer are *Saccharomyces cerevisiae* (ale yeast), and *S. pastorianus* (lager yeast). Though scientists consider these two strains to be basically the same, brewers distinguish the two based on how each behaves in wort. Ale yeast ferments rather quickly, and creates a wide variety of esters that can add an enormous amount of flavor to beer. Slower-fermenting lager yeast seems to prefer the bottom of the vessel, and consumes a greater variety and proportion of malt sugars producing few to no esters, and a little bit of sulfur during fermentation. Notwithstanding, the two yeast strains require different climates to function and affect potency and flavor in different ways. Before we get into those differences, let's take a quick look at the fermentation process.

FERMENTATION

There are four major stages in the life of a wort-bound yeast cell: lag period, respiration and growth, fermentation, and flocculation and sedimentation. Once packaged yeast enters the cooled wort, it is fragile, hungry, and vulnerable. During the lag period, enzymes are secreted that make the cell walls of the yeast permeable. Water and nutrients, including oxygen, are absorbed into the cell's interior. During the second stage, the yeast consumes all available oxygen and, like most living organisms, uses it for energy. Once healthy, the oval yeast cells form small bumps that grow into new cells and break off. Soon, the primordial wort is swimming with hungry, healthy yeast cells, looking for oxygen to continue respiration.

▲ Dry yeast granules—living yeast cells that have been dehydrated into tiny pellets.

▼ Brewer's yeast tablets are often used as a vitamin and mineral supplement and are sold at heath food stores.

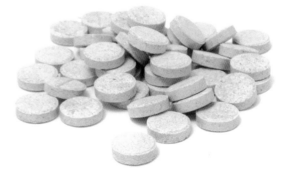

Since the first generation has depleted the oxygen resource, the yeast exercises an anaerobic form of respiration: fermentation. Here, sugars are pillaged for energy, and the yeast excretes two major by-products: ethyl alcohol and carbon dioxide. Eventually, the tiring yeast cells clump together (flocculate) and become inactive. This is the final stage of the process.

The ability of yeast to ferment sugars into alcohol is called attenuation. A typical yeast strain will convert about 70–75 percent of all fermentable material in the wort. Factors that influence this percentage include type of yeast used, amount pitched, amount of oxygen in the wort at pitching time, and fermentation conditions.

ALE YEAST VS LAGER YEAST

Ales have a complex, "rough-around-the-edges" quality that many people enjoy. This is largely due to the quick-fermenting ale yeast. It thrives in warmer temperatures, metabolizes faster, and produces more by-products than its cold-climate counterpart. Also, because it ferments a narrower scope of malt sugars, ales of similar malt content leave more body-enhancing carbohydrates than lagers do.

Ale yeast works best within a temperature range of 60–72°F (16–22°C). Excessively cool temperatures cause cells to go dormant, that is, to settle into a state of inactive "hibernation." Conversely, high temperatures can result in undesirable flavors. Be careful to avoid sudden drops or rises in temperature. All yeast needs stable climactic conditions. Don't store your fermenter near an open window or a heating duct.

▶ Ales and lagers are distinct colors.

▲ Different forms of packaged yeast.

Lager yeast thrives at temperatures of 40–56°F (4–13°C). Unless you have a time-share at a German ice cave, you'll need a refrigerator to maintain this temperature range. Lagers also require two-stage fermentation. During the first stage, fermentation is encouraged at the high end of the temperature scale, or even at ale temperatures. The beer is then transferred into a secondary fermenter (ideally a glass carboy) and allowed to continue fermenting and conditioning at gradually decreased temperatures. This means lagers take longer to produce than ales. While an ale may be ready for consumption within as little as

2 weeks, lagers can require up to 3 weeks in the secondary. Some high-gravity lagers, such as Marzen or Oktoberfest, benefit from extended lagering periods—3 months is not unheard of on a commercial scale. The result of lagering is a generally cleaner-tasting, more highly attenuated beer.

Again, the distinction between ale and lager yeast is nebulous. As a novice, stick to quality-brand yeast that contains information relating to style and use on the package. Also, ask other brewers about the performance of specific brands and strains. Finally, experiment, experiment, experiment!

YEAST FORMS: DRY VS LIQUID

Once upon a time, American homebrewers were constrained to inferior ingredients. Those who practiced civil disobedience during Prohibition had to furtively assemble baking elements to concoct their fermented refreshments. Hence, the homebrewer of the 1920s was not unlike the ancient Egyptian.

The legalization of homebrewing prompted higher-quality yeast, and the popularity of this hobby ensures the continuation of this trend. Today, homebrewers have access to two forms of yeast: dry and liquid. Each form can be and is used to make great beer, but there are some differences in how they are used.

DRY YEAST

This form of yeast is widely used because of its ease of use. Dry yeast is simply living yeast cells that have been dehydrated into tiny granules. To ensure purity and vitality, dry yeast should be fresh and completely sealed in a proper package. Yeast packets that are affixed to the bottom of prehopped beer "kits" are unreliable.

Here is a simple method for rehydrating and pitching dry yeast. Boil about ½ cup (110 ml) water and allow it to cool to the temperature of your wort. Sprinkle the yeast into the water and allow it to stand until it forms a mushy soup known as slurry. Pour the slurry into the cooled wort and, with a sanitized spoon, stir briskly for several minutes to introduce oxygen. Cap the fermenter, affix an airlock, and store the wort at the appropriate temperature. Always maintain sanitary conditions when you are doing this!

LIQUID YEAST

The advantage liquid yeast has over dry yeast is there is a much wider variety of liquid yeasts available to homebrewers than dry yeasts. Liquid yeast usually comes in a "smack pack." Inside the pack is a small volume of yeast and a smaller pouch containing sterilized wort. When the pouch is broken, the yeast cells have a safe environment in which to strengthen and multiply.

The drawback to this form is that the yeast is perishable and must be kept refrigerated, and that some time is needed for the prepared packet to become viable. There are also considerably fewer yeast cells per liquid packet. Some homebrewers compensate by using two liquid packets, or creating a yeast starter (see page 135). It is my opinion that one packet is sufficient for low- to medium-gravity worts, if the wort is sufficiently aerated. For higher gravities (>1.060) the above adjustments are a good way to ensure your yeast completes a full and healthy fermentation.

Prepare the liquid yeast packet a day or two before you plan to brew. With the palm of your hand, rupture the inside packet and knead the contents. Store the pack in an area away from excessive heat and light at temperatures between 74–80°F (23–7°C).

At pitching, maintain sanitary conditions. This is crucial when using liquid yeast, because the yeast population will be small at the outset, and vulnerable to bacterial competition. Thoroughly aerate the wort. The introduction of oxygen to the cooled wort is absolutely crucial for a healthy fermentation. With sanitized scissors, snip a corner of the packet and pour in the contents. Quickly cap the fermenter and store it in a dark environment at temperatures recommended on the label of the packet.

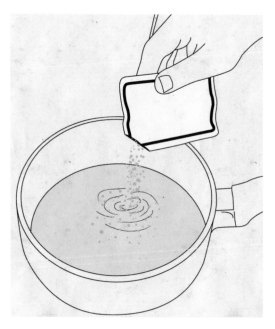

1. *Boil about ½ cup (4 fl oz/110 ml) of water and allow it to cool to about 95ºF (35ºC). Sprinkle the yeast into the water.*

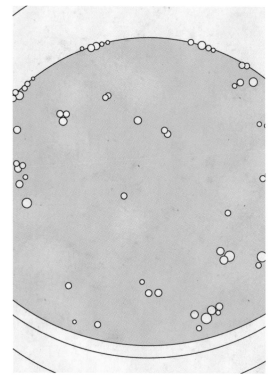

2. *Allow it to stand until it forms a mushy soup known as a slurry.*

WATER

Beer is about 90–95 percent water. In its purest form, water is simply composed of two hydrogen atoms bonded to a single oxygen atom. However, this vital element is filled with varying amounts of mineral and organic matter. Normal drinking water is treated to eliminate most organic compounds, and to regulate the amount of minerals drawn from the raw source. Depending on geographical locale and method of treatment, your water may range from soft to hard. Besides heating and filtration, water treatment plants often add a little chlorine to ensure that the water from your faucet is safe to drink (i.e. sanitary). Tap water that smells and tastes good is fine for the purposes of malt-extract brewing. Professional brewers and homebrewers who use grains tend to be more concerned with what minerals are in their water source. Why?

A CLOSER LOOK AT WATER

While pure water is chemically expressed as H_2O, most water contains dissolved minerals. This is because H_2O has a slight positive and negative electrical charge, and therefore attracts mineral compounds with similar electric charges. For example, table salt (NaCl, or sodium chloride) dissolves in water because each ion in the mineral compound has an electrical charge that corresponds with the charges in H_2O.

Certain dissolved minerals or "salts" aid in the brewing process in a number of ways. Some help make brew liquor more acidic, which is needed for malt starch conversion during the mash. Others help break down ingredients that would otherwise fall out of solution and, therefore, contribute nothing to the final brew. Still others enhance aroma and flavor characteristics proffered by the ingredients, or contribute qualities of their own.

Only specially treated water is free of mineral ions. All naturally drawn water contains varying amounts of ions, depending on where it comes from and how it's been treated. Indeed, these differences dictate the style and characteristics of beer produced around the world. It's no accident that pale ale was perfected at English breweries that drew their waters from Burton upon Trent. The source is naturally rich in calcium sulfate (gypsum), which influences hop isomerization and enhances bitterness perception, resulting in a firm, dry beer. The low mineral content of the waters in the Czech Republic helped the Pilsner lager obtain its world-famous soft, rounded flavor and distinctive hop aroma. Clearly, when the professional brewer wishes to replicate a famous style of beer, he or she is very concerned with water chemistry.

▶ One of the best ways to learn about different beer styles is by ordering a sampler or "flight" of beers.

WATER AND THE MALT-EXTRACT BREWER

As an extract brewer, you needn't be overly concerned with your water. Malt extract is a professionally mashed wort that contains proper mineral levels. You are beginning at a stage after most of the ions have done their work, and quality beer can be produced using good, clean water.

There are three main considerations the novice brewer should understand when choosing brew water:

1. The water is safe for human consumption
2. The water is free from a heavy iron or metallic flavor
3. The water is free of chlorine aromas or flavors

Tap water must be safe, i.e., free of pathogens and other microorganisms. Water plants use filtering techniques to rid water of most organic material. Chlorine is often added to further ensure potability and to keep microscopic bugs from entering the water. The low levels at which it is added mean it is safe for humans but toxic to microbes. However, if your water smells or tastes of chlorine, measures should be taken to remove it, as it could negatively affect the flavor and head-retention of your homebrew. This is easily accomplished by either letting the water stand in an open bucket for 24 hours, or boiling it for 10 minutes prior to adding extract. Activated carbon water filters are increasingly popular. Some filters attach directly to your faucet and others are built into pitchers. A carbon filter will rid your water of most chlorine compounds.

If your water has a metallic flavor, it is probably the result of old or rusty pipes. If this is the case, use bottled drinking water.

Keep in mind that your water can be contaminated during the brewing process. Proper sanitation of all materials that come into contact with the wort is a must. This is extremely important to remember once your kettle leaves the heat source. Cooled wort and water additions to the fermenter must be kept as sanitary as possible.

POPULAR BREWING SALTS

Even as an extract brewer, you can enhance certain characteristics of your brew with the addition of certain salts. The following are cheap, accessible additives that you can add to your extract wort:

Gypsum (calcium sulfate) Half to one teaspoon of gypsum per 5 gallons (23 liters) of brew will aid in clarification, and will sharpen the perceived bitterness of your beer. Gypsum is recommended for IPAs, pale ales, and stouts. It is less often used in lager.

Table salt (sodium chloride) Small additions can accentuate perceived flavors from other ingredients and give your brew a soft, rounded flavor. Table salt should be used sparingly ($^1/_2$ tsp or less) and probably should not be used in conjunction with gypsum at the novice level. Excess levels of sodium and sulfate can cause an unpleasant harshness, quite unlike the bitterness of a well-balanced brew.

For now, as long as your water source is safe and tastes good, let water be the least of your concerns. Concentrate instead on using fresh ingredients, practicing proper technique, and thoroughly cleaning and sanitizing all equipment prior to use.

▲ Table salt added in small amounts can give your brew a soft, rounded flavor.

▼ Gypsum is recommended for IPAs, pale ales, and stouts to help clarification.

ADJUNCTS AND OTHER ADDITIVES

Anyone who holds sacred the German purity law of 1516 should probably skip this section. Here you will find oats, rye, brown sugar, invert sugar, and unmalted grains—enough stuff to make the Elector of Bavaria shudder in his grave. Some American microbreweries hold their adherence to the Reinheitsgebot like a flag; but still others see a wide array of unexplored flavors, textures, and characteristics waiting to be used.

Remember that you are the artist and beer is your work in progress. You have access to a limitless array of ingredients. My advice is to experiment and have fun.

ADJUNCTS

This is a term for any source of sugar used to make beer that is not malted barley. Adjuncts include oat or rye flakes, corn, rice, and unmalted barley. They will often be treated for use in brewing. One problem homebrewers encounter using flaked grains is thickening of the wort. To avoid this, keep additions small, and steep them in as much water as your pot can safely hold (remember—leave some headspace for the boil!).

SUGARS

While mashing converts complex carbohydrates into sugars, many types of sugar can be added directly to the wort.

▲ Many adjuncts, like wheat, come in many forms. This is flaked wheat (left) and torrified wheat (right).

◀ Caramel is a sugar product that can contribute innovative and delicious qualities to your homebrew.

Corn sugar (glucose) is often used for priming homebrew. This simple sugar is completely fermentable, and will boost the potency of your beer. It will also, however, produce a thin, cidery brew if used in any great quantity. Corn sugar is like nitroglycerin. A small amount before bottling will get your yeast pumping, but too much at any time will prove unreliable and potentially explosive.

Some sugars are necessary for the accurate replication of a particular style. Many Trappist brews contain invert and/or candi sugar to add alcohol content and flavor without body. Other sugar products include treacle, molasses, caramel, and beet sugar. While each of these sugars contributes its own unique qualities to various styles of beer, keep experimental levels low until you know exactly how each will react in your homebrew.

FRUITS AND SPICES

Fruits and spices are used to add additional flavor to homebrew. Fruits such as cherries, raspberries, peaches, blueberries, and apricots can be used as supplements to many styles of brew. Extracts are often available at homebrew supply stores or can be purchased via mail order. Fresh fruit can also be used, but care must be taken to avoid "off" flavors. Pasteurize fresh fruit by heating it to 150–170°F (65–76°C) for about 15 minutes. This, will minimize microbes. Excessive heat will extract pectin from the fruit, causing haze in your beer. Add fruit to a secondary fermenter only when yeast activity has slowed. Buckets are ideal for fruit additions, since they allow more headspace for the sugary produce to churn and foam. Also, fine-mesh nylon steeping bags will hold your fruit in one place, making siphoning easier. After two weeks, rack the mixture, without the fruit chunks, into a carboy.

Spices such as cinnamon, coriander, spruce, or licorice—the list goes on and on—can be added to your homebrew. Generally small amounts of these can be added during the final 15 minutes of your boil. Use spices with care, and always add in small additions until you understand how each affects the flavor of your final homebrew.

◀ Fruits such as peaches, blueberries, and cherries can be used to add flavor to your homebrew.

▲ Add fruit to the secondary fermenter in a fine-mesh nylon steeping bag.

FININGS/CLARIFIERS

The following products can be added to your homebrew to aid in clarification. Most work by adhering to such haze-causing substances as suspended proteins, yeast, and carbohydrates, dropping them to the bottom of the brewpot, fermenter, bottle, or keg.

Irish Moss This is a form of seaweed whose active ingredient, carrageenan, is a negatively charged substance that attracts, and drops from suspension, positively charged proteins. Used to prevent "chill haze," add 1 teaspoon during the last 15 minutes of the boil.

Isinglass This is a palatable term for pulverized fish bladders which aid clarification by settling suspended yeast during aging. Don't add during primary fermentation. This is sometimes considered a controversial ingredient due to fishing practices where it is farmed.

Gelatin This is added before bottling to settle suspended matter.

Polyclar This polymer traps suspended proteins in the finished beer and drops them from suspension. Add a few hours before bottling.

CHAPTER 3

EQUIPMENT

The popularity of homebrewing has prompted the emergence of a cornucopia of brewing equipment and gadgetry. What was once a grassroots venture where "equipment" meant a pot, a bucket, and a couple of dozen bottles, has proliferated into a national hobby supported by businesses that supply everything needed to brew professional-quality beer, along with some tech extravagances.

This chapter lists and describes all of the equipment you'll need to brew extract and partial-mash beer. The accessories required to bottle and keg your homebrew are also covered. By this point, you may have acquired a basic kit that has gotten you through a few batches. These "essentials" are detailed here, along with other items that you'll want in order to upgrade your homebrewing system.

Take the time to familiarize yourself with this equipment and explore the advances homebrewing has made in the last decade. Today, the homebrewer has (somewhat) affordable access to nearly every tool enjoyed by the professional brewer. Just remember that making good beer doesn't require every tech advancement out there. Be judicious when building your home brewery. Take it slow. And enjoy.

BREWING EQUIPMENT

BREWPOTS

Brewpots come in a number of sizes and forms. While the novice might need only a 3- or 4-gallon (14–18-liter) saucepan, intermediate and all-grain brewers require vessels for larger volumes of wort. Some of the more popular types are made of stainless steel or enamelware. Some advanced brewers convert commercial kegs into brewpots. This allows them a large, durable vessel that can hold up to 15 gallons (56 liters). These can be purchased through mail-order companies or modified at home.

For performance and affordability, you can't beat stainless steel. It's durable, conductive, and easy to clean. A large saucepan is sufficient for extract brewing. As long as you can boil at least 3 gallons (14 liters) of wort with a few inches of headspace to avoid boil-overs, you're fine.

As you progress into such intermediate steps as partial-mashing and calculated hop scheduling, you'll want a larger pot. These can be found at your local homebrew or restaurant supply store. All-grain brewers often use kettles that accommodate 6 gallons (27 liters) of wort, that eventually boil down to a 5-gallon (23-liter) batch. For the novice and intermediate brewer, this is unnecessary.

A 5- to 7-gallon (23- to 32-liter) stainless-steel pot is practical for the partial-mash brewer. A second, smaller saucepan can be used for the steeping or mashing of any grains that may be added.

▲ A selection of different-sized pans is useful.

▼ Brewpot.

STRAINERS, FUNNELS, AND SPOONS

A large metal strainer is useful during a few stages of the homebrewing process. It is an easy way to withhold hop and trub matter when pouring chilled wort into a fermenter. For the partial-mash brewer, it can be used for sparging grains into the brewpot.

Funnels can be used for pouring cooled wort and yeast slurry into a carboy. A sanitizable plastic funnel is sufficient but stainless steel is better.

A couple of long, sanitizable spoons will prove invaluable. You'll use your spoon to stir the boiling wort, to agitate cooled wort after the yeast is pitched, and to extract items like bags and your floating thermometer.

The best spoons for brewing are stainless steel or food-grade plastic. Wood is not suitable for stirring cooled wort because it is porous and cannot be sanitized.

▲ Spoons.

◀ Funnels.

FERMENTING EQUIPMENT

▲ A plastic fermenting bucket—remember to clean without harsh brushes.

BUCKETS

If you want to use plastic then buy buckets from the homebrew store. Plastic fermentation buckets make fine vessels for quick-fermenting ales, or as primary fermenters. The large opening in the top makes pouring the chilled wort from the brewpot easy, and built-in handles allow simple transportation from kitchen to storage. The buckets are food-grade and have a rubber ring in the lid that assures a tight seal, and also have a predrilled hole in the lid to accept an airlock. Since most have plastic spouts near the bottom of the vessel, liquid is easily transferred to a carboy. Assuming a good cold break and yeast flocculation, most sediment is left behind during transfer because the tap is slightly elevated.

However, because of their slightly porous structure, fermenting beer should not be stored in plastic for more than two or three weeks. Even food-grade plastic contains microscopic holes that tiny microbes can eventually find. In addition, plastic is easily scuffed. This creates niches that can harbor bacteria. Glass carboys are superior for long conditioning times and for lagering. Many homebrewers primary-ferment in plastic but condition in glass.

CARBOYS

These are glass containers ideal for second-stage fermentation or maturation. They are generally obtainable in either 5- or 6½-gallon (23- or 30-liter) sizes. For ales, you can primary-ferment in a bucket and transfer your wort off the sediment into a 5-gallon (23-liter) carboy for maturation. If you use a carboy for primary fermentation, the larger size is recommended.

As long as your carboy is properly sealed with either an airlock or blow-off tube, you can age your beer as long as you like. Glass has an impermeable molecular bond, so you don't have to worry about microbial contamination. This is particularly important in lager brewing, where slow fermentation in a second vessel can require months.

▶ 5- and 6½-gallon carboys.

Glass, however, is fragile. Carboys will not withstand very hot temperatures, and will break if you pour near-boiling wort into an empty vessel. When transferring wort into a carboy make sure either that the wort is cooler than 100°F (38°C) or that there is some cold water in the fermenter to absorb the heat shock.

They also tend to be a bit unwieldy. Be careful when moving a full, heavy carboy, and make sure it is dry. Heavy, unwieldy, and slick—this can make for a potential disaster. At the very least, you'll lose the beer you worked so diligently to craft. You can buy handles that fit around the neck of the carboy. Ask your store owner about his or her experience with these as to how effective they are.

Carboys are also harder to clean and transfer wort from than their plastic counterparts. Always fill your carboy with water immediately after use to loosen any sediment that collects on the bottom and sides. Carboy brushes and bottle-washers are great to scour your carboy.

Transferring wort to a secondary fermenter, or to bottles or a keg, requires the use of tubing, the size and specifications of which are listed on the next page.

▶ Heavy-duty food-grade tubing is needed for blow-off on a 5-gallon carboy.

▼ A glass carboy full of brewing beer—the handle fitted around the neck makes it easier to carry.

TUBING

BLOW-OFF TUBING

This is heavy-duty food-grade tubing with an outside diameter of about $1\frac{1}{4}$ in (3 cm). It can replace the airlock on your carboy by stuffing one sanitized end into the filled, cooled carboy and the other end into a bucket of weak bleach/water solution.

Blow-off tubing is recommended if you are using a 5-gallon (23-liter) carboy for primary fermentation. The advantage here is that some of the undesirable compounds produced early may be expelled. Also, whereas airlocks can pop off carboys under the pressure of escaping gases. This is not really a concern if you are using a plastic bucket.

TRANSFER TUBING

This is cheap, easily obtainable, and essential at all levels of brewing. The best place to find the proper-size tubing ($\frac{3}{8}$ in/0.9 cm outside diameter, $\frac{5}{16}$ in/0.8 cm inside diameter) is at your local homebrew supply store. I recommend purchasing 6-ft (180-cm) and 3 ft (90 cm) lengths of tubing.

The longer piece can be used for transfer from one vessel to another and for bottling from a carboy. The shorter one can be directly attached to your plastic fermenter spigot for bottling.

As with all equipment, keep your tubing clean, and sanitize it before use. If it's old, scuffed, or permanently stained, buy more. It's a worthwhile couple of dollars spent.

MEASURING DEVICES

THERMOMETER

The extract brewer will use a thermometer to determine when the wort is cool enough for pitching. The thermometer takes on more importance with the addition of specialty and mashing grains. Since it is important to keep a certain temperature range during the steeping of grains, you'll want a thermometer that can be kept in the pot for frequent readings—it must be able to withstand boiling temperatures.

Meat and dairy thermometers are useful. You can pick up a floating thermometer at any homebrew store. These are nice because they can stay in the pot during the entire process, eliminating the need for resanitation.

Many supply stores sell heat-sensitive sticker thermometers for your fermenter. By checking this "thermometer," you can make necessary adjustments to raise or lower the wort temperature.

TRIPLE-SCALE HYDROMETER

This device is used to measure attenuation, or the degree to which the yeast converts wort sugars into alcohol. This is helpful in gauging when fermentation has ceased. If the hydrometer reads the same number two days in a row, primary fermentation is complete. Hydrometers read in three scales: specific gravity, degrees Plato, and alcohol percentage. The most commonly used and referred-to scale by homebrewers is specific gravity. Hydrometers measure the density of a liquid against the density of water. A hydrometer immersed in water at 60°F (16°C) will read 1.000 specific gravity. Any solids into the water (like sugar!) increase its density, so the hydrometer will rise.

Wort is denser than water, but alcohol is lighter than wort. During fermentation, as the yeast convert sugars into alcohol, the density will drop. Therefore, the first reading (original gravity) will be higher than the last reading (final gravity).

◀ A wine thief or turkey baster can be used to extract wort from your carboy fermenter so you can take a hydrometer reading. It must be cleaned and sanitized.

The Plato scale measures the amount of sucrose by weight in a solution. While there are many sugars in wort, sucrose provides the highest increase in specific gravity. This scale measures the amount of sucrose conversion.

You can also gauge the potency of your brew by taking an initial and final reading of the alcohol scale. Subtract the final number from the original, and you have the alcohol by weight.

A beaker and stand can be purchased at most supply stores for use with the hydrometer.

MEASURING CUP/SCALE

Both of these are used to measure the addition of ingredients. The scale can be used to measure the weight of added hops and other ingredients, and the measuring cup can be used for the addition of priming sugar. Of the two, the measuring cup is more useful. Most homebrew stores have scales on the premises, and ingredients are often packaged in convenient sizes.

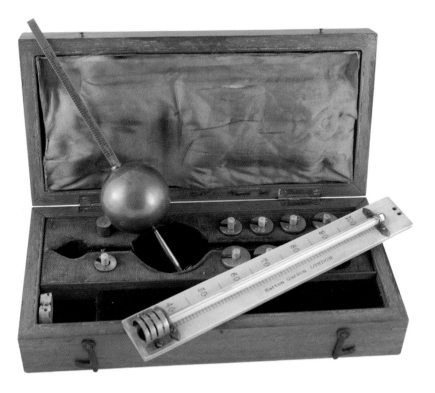

▲ A Sikes hydrometer, used to measure the proof or alcohol content of liquids. A thermometer mounted on a bone plate and a brass float with weight-disks was used to assess the specific gravity of the test liquid, and this was converted to proof with a table and slide rule.

WORT CHILLERS AND OTHER COOL STUFF

IMMERSION WORT CHILLERS

An immersion wort chiller is a 20–30 ft (6–9 m) length of copper tubing that is coiled into a stack. The chiller goes in the wort and cold water runs through the copper tubing, cooling the beer. This can bring 5 gallons (23 liters) of near-boiling wort down to pitching temperatures in as little as 15–20 minutes. While immersion wort chillers should be regularly cleaned, you can sanitize yours by placing it in the brewpot for the last 20 minutes of the boil. Incidentally, copper ions that end up in your brew act as yeast nutrients.

COUNTERFLOW WORT CHILLERS

Counterflow wort chillers are more expensive and require more attention. The most basic of these are 15–20 ft (4.5–6 m) of copper tubing inside slightly shorter rubber tubing. More complex versions resemble the plate chillers seen in small breweries. With a few special attachments, the hot wort passes through in one direction as cold water pumps through in the opposite direction, rapidly chilling the wort. The chiller must be cleaned and sanitized after each use. If cared for properly, the counterflow system is superior to the immersion chiller. First, counterflow chillers cool the wort in a closed environment. This means that your wort is insulated against airborne bacteria and yeast. Counterflow chillers also cool faster.

Experiment with a number of techniques before making any large investments. Some homebrewers find that simply placing the brewpot in a sink filled with ice water, or creating a siphon system, is sufficient for cooling purposes. Start with some simple methods and log their efficacy. Record how long it takes to cool your wort to

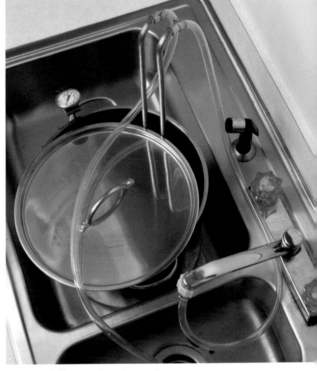

▲ Wort chillers quicken the cooling process.

pitching temperatures. Also note any possible avenues for contamination that your system allows. Work your way up from simple to complex, slowly.

REFRIGERATOR

A spare refrigerator is almost a necessity for lagering beer. It can also be converted into a kegging system. Hunt down used refrigerators at garage sales or in the classified ads.

GAS BURNERS AND OTHER HOT ITEMS

At some point, you may find that your kitchen stove isn't doing the trick. Flame boils water faster, and it is easier to maintain consistent temperatures. Even if you have a gas burner, you'll notice that it won't heat large volumes of wort to boiling quickly. Kitchen ranges also don't accommodate large brewpots very well. Luckily, you can take it outdoors!

OUTDOOR PROPANE COOKERS

These are freestanding steel burners that connect to an ordinary propane tank (like the one used for gas grills) via heavy-duty tubing. These relatively inexpensive devices will accommodate large vessels, and put out a lot of heat. Most will bring 5 gallons (23 liters) of water to a full boil in 10 minutes. Just as you wouldn't dream of bringing your gas grill into the kitchen, don't even consider using a gas burner indoors. Propane is a toxic, highly flammable gas, and should be used only in a well-ventilated area. Make sure all fittings are secure, and check for leaks by spraying a little soapy water around suspect areas. If you see any bubbling, you've got a leak.

ELECTRIC ELEMENTS

It is also possible to mount an open electrical element, similar to a tea kettle, in a plastic or metal brewpot. The main advantage of this over an open fire burner is that they can be used indoors in relative safety. The element itself is subject to a build-up of various deposits, and so should be removed for thorough cleaning at the end of a brew—after it has cooled.

▲ Gas burner and propane tank.

▲ Add the wort chiller to the wort 15–20 minutes before the end of the boil to sanitize it.

INGREDIENT ACCESSORIES

STEEPING BAGS

Some brewers steep their cracked specialty grains in the main brewpot prior to the introduction of malt extract. For this, there are nylon and cloth bags widely available at most supply stores.

STORAGE CONTAINERS

If you want to store extra grain for your next batch, try using an airtight plastic container. Store in a cool dry area, since moisture and exposure to air will encourage microbial and possibly even visible critter infestation.

Hops can be stored in plastic bags in the freezer for a few months. Just make sure all the air is squeezed out and the bags are tightly sealed.

▲ Muslin and grain steeping bags.

GRAIN MILLS

Any grains added to the wort must be gently cracked prior to use. This exposes the modified kernel to the heated water, which will absorb and convert the sugars and starches therein. There is a degree of specificity involved. If you don't crack the grain husks enough, little "goodness" will be extracted. If you grind the grains too much, husk material may find its way into the boil, resulting in a hazy, astringent-tasting brew. The perfect mill crushes the kernel (endosperm) leaving the husk whole and intact, so that it will serve as a filter bed during sparging and not enter the wort.

Many homebrew supply stores sell precrushed grains or have grain mills on the premises. If you want to use the latter, be sure that all the debris is cleared out of the mill. You don't want the powdery remains of someone else's grain in your bag. The alternative is to purchase your own grain mill. While this is more of a concern for all-grain brewers who use large amounts of malt, the specialty and partial-mash malt-extract brewer may find these devices helpful. Several models are available.

Coffee grinders can be used, with some success, by extract-brewers who wish to add small amounts of specialty grain. Keep in mind, however, that the primary function of these devices is to grind coffee grains. Therefore, they can't be relied upon to crack barley with any consistency. Often, a good portion of the husk is pulverized along with the endosperm. If you have a coffee grinder at home, try using it only for specialty grain additions. Place the grains in a grain bag to minimize the addition of husk material.

The Corona mill has long been a staple in the all-grain brewer's arsenal, although its efficacy as the right tool for the job is questionable. This is a simple, hand-cranked unit that is definitely a step up from the coffee grinder. The Corona mill was originally designed to grind corn, although it can be adjusted to accept barley. Some all-grain brewers have devised systems that allow the use of a hand-held drill to replace the manual crank, and have constructed add-on boxes that allow a greater amount of malt to be fed into the grinder at once. Again, it is perhaps no substitute for buying professionally ground malt, but some people like to get their hands dirty.

Homebrewing roller mills attempt to replicate processional mills with varying degrees of success. Unlike the grinding action of the above tools, roller mills utilize rollers made of cold-rolled steel to draw in and burst the malt. This leaves the husk intact while crushing the endosperm.

When considering the above, my advice is to start cheap and work your way up. There is no reason why you should spend a lot of money on a top-notch roller mill if you're simply adding some specialty grains to your wort. Try purchasing precrushed grains, or use the homebrew supply store mill, if yours has one. Again, concentrate on technique. Once you are confident that your procedures are sound, then start shopping around for more expensive equipment.

▲ The Corona grain mill, a useful gadget for the homebrewer.

FILTERING AND SANITIZING EQUIPMENT

WATER FILTERS

All municipal water is treated with some level of chlorine. While an excess of this chemical will give your water a "swimming pool" taste, a certain amount is needed to keep the water source sanitary. If you can smell and taste the chlorine in your water, chances are you'll smell and taste it in your beer. In Chapter 2, three methods were offered for dechlorinating your brew water: allowing your water to stand overnight in a open container, preboiling your brew water for 10 minutes before adding ingredients, or by using Campden tablets. Each of these procedures will eliminate most of the chlorine in your water.

▼ A carbon-activated water filter in action.

An easier and more effective method is to employ a charcoal (carbon) filter. These connect directly to your faucet and eliminate all traces of chlorine and chlorine compounds. A high-quality filter may seem a little expensive, but will last a long time. If you find you are resorting to bottled water for every batch because you can't get rid of the chlorine taste, consider a filter.

BEER FILTERS

Some people argue that any cloudiness is the sign of an inferior brew. There is some truth in this. Certain bacterial infections can cause strange-looking beers (the corresponding tastes are even stranger), and an excess of suspended proteins and sugars can cast a haze over your chilled homebrew. Still, for many styles of beer—for example, many wheat ales—a little cloudiness is expected. It's worth remembering that if your brewing practices are sound and sanitary, a slight haze will be no bad thing, and removing it may actually remove flavor compounds too.

For those who want to rid their beer of haze, there are filters that will remove the materials. Two popular types of filters are cartridge and plate filters. Both require a CO_2 tank to force the beer through tiny holes that trap yeast, bacteria, and protein-tannin molecules. There are inserts for each of these filters that provide various degrees of filtration. The pores range from 5–0.5 microns in diameter. Considering that one micron is one-thousandth of a millimeter, you can imagine how small these pores are.

On a microscopic level, yeasts are the big fish in the sea. Consequently, they are often the first to be caught in the tiny net of filtration. However, you need yeast in your

▲ There are different types of water filters available to purchase.

bottle if you want to achieve carbonation through conditioning. There are systems that allow you to artificially carbonate bottled beer, but this complicates matters further. Filters work best with kegged beer, which can be easily carbonated by forcing gas into solution via a CO_2 tank.

CLEANERS AND SANITIZERS

There is a difference between cleaning and sanitizing. You can't sanitize equipment that you haven't yet cleaned, and clean equipment cannot be used until it is sanitized. Clean equipment is well scrubbed and free of any spots, stains, and residues. Since bacteria can establish thriving communities in the smallest bits of residue, these must be eliminated before you take measures to evict any rogue microbes. Sanitation is not the same as

sterilization. A sterile environment is impossible to achieve, except under confined laboratory conditions. Sterilization is both impractical and unnecessary for the homebrewer. Sanitation is the removal of most harmful bacteria and wild yeast, and can be easily achieved with the proper tools and chemicals. The following is a list of such items.

BOTTLE BRUSH/CARBOY BRUSH

These are used with water and cleaning/ sanitizing compounds to loosen and remove stuck-on residues. Swishing water in your mouth won't remove stubborn particles; likewise spraying and soaking bottles and carboys won't rid the containers of accumulated sediments. In both cases a stiff-bristled brush will wipe those deposits away. Carboy brushes are longer than bottle brushes, and are often bent at an angle so you can scrub the inside of the neck.

▼ Carboy and bottle brushes are useful for cleaning glass, but do not use on plastics.

CLEANERS/SANITIZERS TIPS

Your local homebrew shop will carry a myriad of cleaners and sanitizers available for use with your homebrew equipment. Some can be hard on stainless steel equipment, so be sure to check with the staff to find out what's right for you. As with any cleaner or sanitizer, read the instructions, dose rate, and active temperature carefully and be sure to use proper protective equipment when using caustics and acids at home. Some of these chemicals are designed to break down organic materials quickly. Be sure to protect your hands and face at all times.

Commercial oxidants clean and, to some degree, sanitize your equipment. The recommended ratio is 1 tablespoon mixed with 1 gallon (4.5 liters) of water. These are great soaking agents and they won't damage metals. I often keep my empty kegs filled with one of these cleaners. Both loosen "beer stone" (hardened sediment) and keep kegs clean and ready to sanitize. While most of these are environmentally friendly, you'll need to rinse each piece of equipment after soaking in these solutions. You should read the manufacturer's instructions carefully, as the directions of use for each product could vary slightly.

- Star San is an acid-based foaming sanitizer that sanitizes on contact without soaking. At lower (but effective) concentrations, it can be used as a no-rinse agent.

- Remember that if you rinse a sanitizer off, you should do so with sanitized or sterilized water so as to not recontaminate what was just sanitized.

▲ Bottle trees are perfect for drying sanitized bottles.

VINEGAR AND OTHER PRODUCTS

Vinegar (acetic acid) This can be used to clean copper equipment. Use white distilled vinegar. This is great for taking the tarnish off an immersion wort chiller. Just make sure you thoroughly rinse off all of the vinegar before you place it in your wort.

Grain alcohol Dilute this with water for cleaning and sanitizing counters and tables. Fill a spray bottle with one part alcohol per five parts water, and mist and wipe surfaces.

Iodophor You can use this to clean stainless-steel equipment, without fear of corrosion. If used in the correct dilution, it is a no-rinse sanitizer. Wear old clothing when using as this cleaner can stain. The recommended potency is $\frac{1}{2}$ oz (14 g) per 5 gallons (23 liters) water.

Oven cleaner This can be used to remove carbon buildup on the bottom of your brewpot. Be sure to dilute the caustic agent with water. White distilled vinegar works well.

Heating equipment Temperatures above 170°F (77°C) kill microorganisms. This method works well for metal objects.

▼ Clean all surfaces with a dilute bleach/water solution.

BOTTLING

BOTTLES

Your best bet is brown, cap-top bottles. Clear and green bottles allow light in. This can react with hops and create "skunky" flavors. Screw-top bottles cannot be resealed, and the glass will not withstand gas pressures during conditioning.

You may also come across bottles that have swing-top plastic or ceramic resealable tops. These make bottling a breeze. Just make sure you have a supply of rubber seals to replace the old ones with when they become dry and cracked.

▲ A brewer fills a bottle from the bottling bucket using a bottling tip.

BOTTLE CAPPER

There is a wide variety of bottle cappers available on the market. The cheapest is the hammer capper. The reason it's cheap is that it is difficult to use and can break bottles. The next level is the two-handed capper. These are easy to use and relatively inexpensive. This is the kind of capper that is included in most kits.

If you plan on bottling beer for many years, you'll want to invest in a bench capper. It should be adjustable to accommodate bottles of various sizes. These are so easy to use that they can actually make bottling fun.

▶ Bench and "Emily" type bottle cappers for your homebrew.

BOTTLE FILLER AND RACKING CANE

A bottle filler is a plastic stem that connects to your fermenter via tubing. The tip has a spring-activated point that allows beer to flow from fermenter to bottle when pressed.

A racking cane is used during bottling and wort transfers. It is a hard, cane-shaped pipe that extends to the bottom of a carboy or bucket. Unlike soft tubing, a racking cane won't crimp (but will break if you try to bend it too hard) so that beer can flow freely. There is also a cap at the straight end with an opening $1/2$ in (1 cm) up, to discourage sediment.

▶ Caps are available from homebrew supply stores or online.

CO$_2$ TANK AND PRESSURE REGULATOR

Homebrewers often use 5-gallon (23-liter) CO$_2$ tanks because they can fit inside small refrigerators and are cheap to fill. Some homebrewers prefer 20-gallon (90-liter) tanks because they cut down on the number of trips made to the gas supplier. Check with beverage distributors for used tanks. When you purchase a used tank, it's a good idea to get it professionally pressure-tested. Visual inspections and hydrostatic tests determine whether a tank is safe for use. If an inspector detects any flaws on the internal aluminum canister, he or she will empty the tank and drill a hole in it. Since these tanks hold anywhere from 800–4,000 lb (360–1,800 kg) of pressurized air per square inch (5 sq cm), it is essential that they are safe.

A pressure regulator controls the force of gas from the tank. Most have two gauges attached; one shows the amount of gas in the tank, and the other shows how much pressure is entering your keg. Attach your regulator to the out-valve of your tank by screwing the threaded nut over the valve. There should be a plastic gasket inside the casing to assure a secure seal. You can control the flow of CO$_2$ by turning a screw on the side.

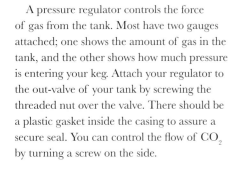

2. Hook up the tap line.

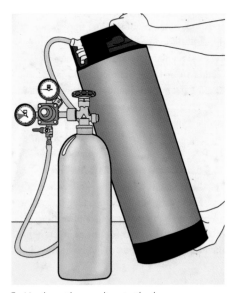

1. Hook up the gas line to the keg.

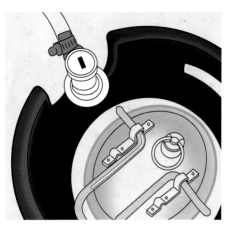

3. Force-carbonate your beer.

KEG CONDITIONING AND DISPENSING

Procedures for conditioning in a keg are essentially the same as those for the bottle. The only difference is that you'll be using less priming sugar. If a recipe calls for 5 oz (150 g) corn sugar for bottles, use $2\frac{1}{2}$ oz (65 g) in the keg.

QUICK CARBONATION

With a little muscle and some CO_2, you can carbonate your homebrew without using priming sugar. By forcing gas into your flat beer, you can have bubbly beer in less than two days. First, cool your beer and transfer it into a sanitized keg. Hook the keg up to the tank and set the regulator to 25 psi. Pull the release valve on the keg to replace the air on the surface with CO_2. Shake the keg for about a minute. You should hear gas groaning through the regulator. This gas is being absorbed into your beer. Repeat shaking two more times, or until the sound ceases. Unhook your keg, turn off the tank, and leave for a day or two.

DISPENSING FROM THE KEG

Connect your keg to the gas and tap lines. Set your regulator to 8 psi. Your first glass or two of beer may be cloudy. Pour a clear glass and check the carbonation. If your beer is flat, disconnect it from the tap and check for leaks. Once you are sure the keg is well sealed, force-carbonate again.

Ideally, you want a steady flow of beer, one that allows a head to form but doesn't shoot from the tap. At the end of the day, either disconnect the gas line from the keg and turn off the tank, or close the valve on your regulator.

▲ You can easily install a beer tap at home for that authentic bar feel.

REFRIGERATORS/"KEGERATORS"

Now you have all the basic hardware to dispense your homebrew—all you need is some way to cool your brew. An inexpensive and portable option is to construct a "jockey box." This is a picnic cooler that is connected inline between your keg and the tap by a length of winding copper tubing set inside. The cooler is filled with ice, which cools the beer as it flows from the keg to glass. Several books and Internet sources provide instructions for constructing one of these handy devices.

A more effective, if stationary, system is to find an old refrigerator in the classified section of your local newspaper. Any refrigerator that can maintain a temperature range of 40–48°F (4–9°C) is suitable. Remove plastic shelving, and be sure the inside floor can withstand the weight of a full keg and tank. Scrub any mold from the interior, and wipe with a sanitizing agent. Then drill a hole in the door of the unit, feed your tap through, and seal the deal with silicone caulk.

Small refrigerators and freezers also make nice cooling units for your system—just make sure you can fit your keg and CO_2 tank inside. If the interior space prohibits this, you can arrange your tank outside the unit and feed the gas line through a drilled hole in the side.

Many small refrigerators contain freezer compartments that cut down on the internal space. The metal box can be removed and flipped around, giving you the headspace you need for your keg. Be sure you know what you're doing if you want to try this, however. It may also be possible to find a local independent refrigeration engineer to modify a small refrigerator that will hold a 5-gallon (23-liter) keg and a 5-gallon (23-liter) CO_2 tank.

Small meat freezers are compact and well insulated, and thus make great dispensing coolers. Often, these have external temperature controllers that you can set to your preference. Since you don't want a "beercicle," you'll want to add a thermostatic controller. Thermostatic controllers can be purchased by mail order, at some hardware stores, and at some homebrew supply stores. These are a good investment if you are using a freezer for dispensing beer, or if you're using a single freezer or refrigerator for the dual purpose of lagering and dispensing homebrew. Most of these devices plug into a wall outlet. By attaching the controller to the side of your unit and placing the wired temperature probe within, you can maintain consistent temperatures.

Whichever electric cooling unit you have, you can upgrade your plastic tap to a more handsome and professional-looking tap handle. You can find taps that can be mounted on either the top or side of your refrigerator. Check with your local homebrew supply store for tap systems.

▲ A draft system using a separate refrigerator.

CHAPTER 4

PREPARING TO BREW

Good preparation is the key to successful homebrewing. This includes:

1. Cleaning and sanitizing all of your equipment
2. Organizing and cleaning your work area
3. Having your ingredients ready for use
4. Making a checklist of all the above steps

Following these steps will improve the quality of your homebrew in several ways. First, the most common source of off flavors and other problems that can plague homebrew is the presence of unwanted microorganisms. The best equipment and the finest, freshest ingredients won't compensate for unsanitary conditions. Sanitation is the foremost concern of the homebrewer. Taking extra time to ensure that all of your equipment is free of contaminants will guarantee clean, great-tasting homebrew. The same goes for your work area. If the area you brew in is dirty and disorganized, you are inviting microbial visitors and ensuring a day of searching and confusion.

Are your ingredients present and accounted for? Running to the store because you don't have the extra corn sugar you thought you had will put stress on you and your brew. If you're using liquid yeast, make sure you've prepared it at least a day in advance. By having all of your ingredients ready and at arm's reach, you'll be ready when the time comes to add them to the pot or fermenter.

Finally, checklisting the above steps will provide assurance that you haven't left anything out. This chapter details each of these procedures, and illustrates how they will improve your homebrew and the fun you have making it.

GETTING ORGANIZED

YOUR WORK AREA

The main work area for the extract brewer is usually the kitchen. Brewers who use propane cookers may use the garage or deck as their boiling area, and then carry the wort into the kitchen to be cooled, transferred, and pitched with yeast. Many brewers store sanitized equipment in the bathtub. Wherever you work, you must clean and, when possible, sanitize. Indoor cleaning includes sweeping and mopping the floor, wiping down countertops with a sanitizing agent, and even misting the area with a sanitizing solution. Organization of your area means removing clutter and gathering all the equipment together, and having it ready for use.

Dirty plates and cups should be washed and put away. Countertops should be cleared of any items that might become obstacles while you are brewing.

You should wipe down the stovetop, countertops, and any other contact surfaces with either a sanitizing solution or a 70:30 percent ratio of isopropyl alcohol.

Misting the room with an isopropyl alcohol solution will help cut down on the number of contaminants adrift in your work area.

The bathtub is a good place to store sanitized equipment. A large sanitary bucket filled with prepared equipment can be set aside in the tub until each tool is needed. Of course, you should scour your bathroom before storing equipment, mist the area with a sanitizing solution, and close the toilet lid.

YOUR INGREDIENTS

Only an unexpected boil-over can match the panic you'll feel if, mid-brew, you suddenly realize you forgot an ingredient, or hadn't prepared it for use. Checklist all of your ingredients. If you're using liquid yeast, prepare the packet at least a day in advance. Make sure your grains are crushed.

Finally, make a checklist of all the above steps, and be sure each is completed before you start to brew.

CLEANING AND SANITIZING YOUR EQUIPMENT

I have explained the difference between cleaning and sanitizing. Cleaning must always come first, as dirty equipment is impossible to sanitize. The best time to clean your equipment is right after you've brewed your latest batch. While this might seem tedious after a day of brewing, it's the best time to attack, since the sediment is still moist and easy to remove.

Clean equipment must be sanitized directly prior to brewing. Sanitary tubing can collect an infectious level of airborne contaminants in a few days, as can the rest of your equipment. Summer months are especially troublesome. During muggy weather the air is thick with wild yeasts and bacteria that could unleash trouble if your equipment is not thoroughly cleaned and sanitized.

There are some compounds that will both clean and sanitize your equipment (if it is relatively clean to begin with), reducing the number of janitorial steps. All of these procedures will be discussed shortly, but first a couple of important distinctions. Sanitation is the removal of most harmful microorganisms. Sterilization is the removal of all living organic material. The latter procedure is impractical and unnecessary. As long as your wort is largely free of microbes, the yeast will effectively starve its competition by draining food and oxygen resources. Then, as the alcohol increases during fermentation, the environment within the fermenter becomes less hospitable to microorganisms. Unsanitary conditions increase microbial competition, which utilizes oxygen and food differently than yeast. Other, less pleasant compounds are formed by bacteria and wild yeast, none of which you want in beer. However, don't be worried about accidentally creating a poisonous brew. There are no known pathogens that can exist in beer. Concentrate on brewing a batch that won't leave a bad taste.

There are two phases of the homebrewing process: the hot side and the cold side. The hot side includes equipment used up to a boil and down to where the wort cools to 140°F (60°C). The heat of an extended boil eliminates microorganisms, but make sure your equipment is free of soap or chemical residues that may impact your brew. During the cold side, sanitation is crucial. Cool wort is a breeding ground for bacteria and wild yeast. Everything that comes into contact with wort or beer below 140°F (60°C) must be sanitized.

Equipment used during the hot side includes the brewpot and lid, stirring spoon, strainer, immersion thermometer, and grain and hops bags. Each of these should be clean and free of any residue before you brew. Here's how to do it.

HOT-SIDE EQUIPMENT

BREWPOT AND LID

Brewpots can be cleaned with a mild, unscented hand-dishwashing detergent and a soft sponge. Stubborn deposits can be removed by filling the brewpot with hot water for an hour and then using a plastic scrubbing pad to dislodge the residue. If gunk in your brewpot is especially tenacious, try soaking it in one of the following mixtures:

Commercial oxidants Most commercial oxidants contain peroxides that break up stubborn organic deposits. These are nontoxic and safe to use on metal. However, rinse off all traces of the slippery residue before use.

The lid can usually be cleaned using a little unscented hand-dishwashing detergent and a sponge. Since both pot and lid will be subjected to high heat, you don't have to worry about sanitation. Just make sure that each is thoroughly rinsed of any residue. Both beer and detergent can foam up, yet the two mixed will create a brew with no foamy head.

After several homebrew sessions, you may notice a slight patina of tarnish developing on the inside of your brewpot. This is not really a concern. It won't negatively affect your beer.

STIRRING SPOON

Wood is not recommended for stirring cool wort, because its porous nature will nurture bacteria. Wood can be used for the hot side, though. So can food-grade plastic and stainless steel. Clean your spoons after each homebrew session, before any gunk can harden on them. A quick washing in warm water before you begin your next batch is sufficient preparation. Try to use brewing spoons only for brewing and keep them clean and free of nicks.

STRAINER

Strainers can be cleaned in the same fashion as the brewpot. If you have reservations about sparging hot liquid through your grains via the strainer, you can sanitize the strainer. If it is made entirely of metal, simply boil it for 15 minutes. You can soak plastic-sided strainers with a dilute solution of bleach water (1 tablespoon per 5 gallons/23 liters). However, all liquid passed through the strainer will eventually be boiled, killing any microorganisms from either the grain or the strainer.

THERMOMETER

Make sure there is no stuck-on debris; the boil will take care of the rest. If you are using a second thermometer for cold-side readings, sanitize it.

GRAIN AND HOPS BAGS

Hops bags are meant to be disposable. Simply fill them with hops, drop them in the wort, and when the time comes, throw the bags away. Nylon grain bags can be reused, but should be cleaned by boiling after each use. Hops bags used for dry hopping must be sanitized; boil the empty bag for 10–15 minutes.

COLD-SIDE EQUIPMENT

Once your wort drops below 140°F (60°C), all conditions and equipment must be sanitary. Some labs actually use malt-extract concentrates to develop strains of microorganisms. The warm, nutritious solution is an ideal environment for cultivation. However, you don't have to don a lab coat to avoid microbial intrusion. Just keep your equipment and space sanitary.

The list of equipment used during the cold side is longer than the one detailing the previous phase. It includes such procedures as wort cooling, transfer into primary and secondary fermenters, yeast pitching, and bottling or kegging. All equipment used for these steps must be sanitary. Perfectly good wort or beer can be spoiled if it comes into contact with a contamination source.

To clean and sanitize equipment used during the cold side, start by carefully inspecting all of your equipment. Pay close attention to detail. Stains, tarnish, and organic residues harbor bacteria that cannot be reached by sanitizing agents. Rid your soiled equipment of these deposits so that they can be properly sanitized. Cleaning usually includes a sponge or pad, a little detergent, and a lot of wiping and scrubbing. However, different materials require different methods. You won't want to use a carboy brush on the soft interior of your bucket, and you can't use a sponge to reach the inside areas of bottles or carboys.

PLASTICS
These include fermentation buckets, transfer and blow-off tubing, racking canes and bottle fillers, spigots, airlocks and rubber stoppers, and plastic stirring spoons. First, make sure none of these items is scratched or nicked. If they are, throw them away. You're investing money, time, and love into your craft, so don't allow hidden bacteria to spoil your brew. Clean your plastic fermenter by wiping it with a sponge soaked in the sanitizing solution. If those stains remain, fill the bucket with a commercial oxidant, and allow the chemicals to do their thing. Any of these can be left in the fermenter for an extended period of time, unless otherwise specified. Next, empty the bucket and wipe out residue. If using commercial oxidants, rinse with hot, then warm, then cold water.

Sanitizing a clean bucket is easy with a half-hour soaking in sanitizing solution. Before you start to brew, pour out the liquid, and replace the lid to stop airborne contaminants from entering.

The lid can be cleaned and sanitized along with the bucket. Wipe it with the sponge, paying special attention to the underside, the airlock hole, and the rubber seal around the inside rim.

If you have a spigot attached to your bucket, you may want to remove it for cleaning and sanitizing. The threads that screw onto the inner gasket can become filled with malt and hop residue. Soak all parts in a cleaner to loosen the sediment. Next, dip a cotton swab into the solution and clean out the grooved surfaces. While you're giving this area particular attention, stick a predipped cotton swab up the nozzle of the spigot to clean its interior. Finally, soak the attachments in another cleaning solution for a half-hour, rinse with sanitized water if desired, and replace it on the bucket.

A vigorous fermentation can belch yeast into your airlock and stain your rubber stopper. Clean rubber stoppers with the above methods.

Plastic tubing can be quite troublesome to maintain. Both the inside and outside of transfer and blow-off tubing are exposed to the brew at some point, so each must be clean and free of pests. The outside can be wiped, but the inside is more difficult to access.

Soak the tubing in a diluted oxidant for an hour or so to loosen any caked-on material. Next, dip a piece of paper towel in the same solution and twist it into a shape that will just fit into one end of the tubing. Using water from either your sink or garden hose (the latter is recommended) force the paper towel through the tubing until it spits out at the other end. Now, repeat this process starting at the opposite end of the tubing. This should rid your hose of debris. Thoroughly rinse the inside and outside of the tubing until all traces of cleaner are gone. If your tubing doesn't squeak when you rub it, it's not completely rinsed. Sanitize the tubing and hang it out to dry.

Your racking cane and bottle filler should be soaked in a sanitizing solution.

GLASS

Glass equipment includes carboys, bottles, thermometers, and hydrometers. You don't need to worry about the last item, because any wort or beer extracted for a hydrometer reading will not be introduced back into the source. Still, you should regularly clean your hydrometer with warm water to keep the scale accurate.

If you're using a separate glass thermometer for post-boil (cold-side) readings it must be clean and sanitary. Clean it as you did for the thermometer used for the boil. Sanitize in a container of sanitizing solution for a half-hour and wipe with a new sponge that has been dipped in the same solution. Keep it in a safe environment until you're ready to take any temperature readings. Keep your hot-side thermometer in the brewpot during all phases of the boil. The same thermometer can be kept in the pot after the

▲ Swing-top growlers are beautiful and an easy way to transport your beer to share with friends.

▲ Commercial breweries spend an enormous time cleaning. To make the best beer at home, clean like the pros: constantly.

boil to monitor the temperature of the cooling wort. Use a second one to measure the temperature of water used for dry yeast rehydration and the temperature of the wort sample used for hydrometer measurement.

You can clean your carboy by filling it with either a commercial oxidant or a cleaning solution, then scrubbing out all organic residues with a carboy brush. Bottle washers are also helpful for "power-washing" the interior surfaces. Sanitize it and let it air-dry. If you rinse the carboy, use cooled, sanitized water as boiling water can crack the glass.

You can store a sanitized carboy indefinitely by placing a piece of aluminum foil over the mouth and securing it with a rubber band.

Bottles can pose a dilemma. Brown bottles are best for storing homebrew, and yet the protection from beer-spoiling light afforded by the brown color also makes it difficult to see deposits that must be removed prior to sanitation. The easiest way to circumvent this problem is to purchase clean, unlabeled bottles at a homebrew supply store and keep them clean by rinsing each one thoroughly after use.

If you obtain bottles from a bar or restaurant, chances are they'll require a lot of cleaning. You should use a bottle washer and a bottle brush to clean the insides. Constant scrubbing and inspection against a strong light will ensure they are free of debris.

Wherever you get your bottles, you'll need to sanitize them before use. Again, a good cleaning solution is important to get rid of any microscopic beasts. You can employ a new plastic trashcan as a holding tank for a couple of dozen bottles. Fill the trashcan three-quarters full of sanitizing solution, and dump your cleaned bottles in. If you are using labeled bottles, you should remove the paper and glue before you put them in the trashcan. In his book *Homebrewing Guide*, Dave Miller suggests using an ice scraper and ammonia to remove labels. This is an effective procedure, but note the following carefully. Make sure all traces of ammonia are rinsed off the bottles before immersing them in chlorine. Chlorine and ammonia produce a toxic gas when mixed! Rinse, rinse, and then rinse the bottles some more. Also, ammonia alone can be unpleasant to work with. Try to remove your labels outside.

On the day you bottle, scoop out all the bottles from the trashcan and allow them to air-dry. Once dry, they are ready to fill.

METAL

Metal equipment used during the cold side includes wort chillers, funnels, spoons, and kegs.

Counterflow wort chillers must be cleaned immediately after use by pumping a large volume of boiling water through the copper lines. Immersion wort chillers can be cleaned using white distilled vinegar and a plastic scrubbing pad. This will keep your copper clean and in mint condition. Be sure to rinse the coils with water to remove any traces of acetic acid. You can sanitize your clean immersion wort chiller by placing it in the brewpot during the last 20 minutes of the boil.

Clean metal funnels using a commercial oxidant. After a brief soaking, scrub the funnel with a plastic scrubbing pad. Sanitize by boiling the funnel in water for 20 minutes, or soaking it in an Iodophor solution.

The easiest way to clean a stainless-steel spoon is to scrub it under warm water. You can sanitize by boiling the metal for 20 minutes. Just be sure not to boil any nonmetallic parts.

Soda kegs can be cleansed using a diluted commercial oxidant. Once the keg is empty, rinse out any residue and fill it with the above-mentioned solution. Store the keg with the lid secured until it's time to keg your next batch.

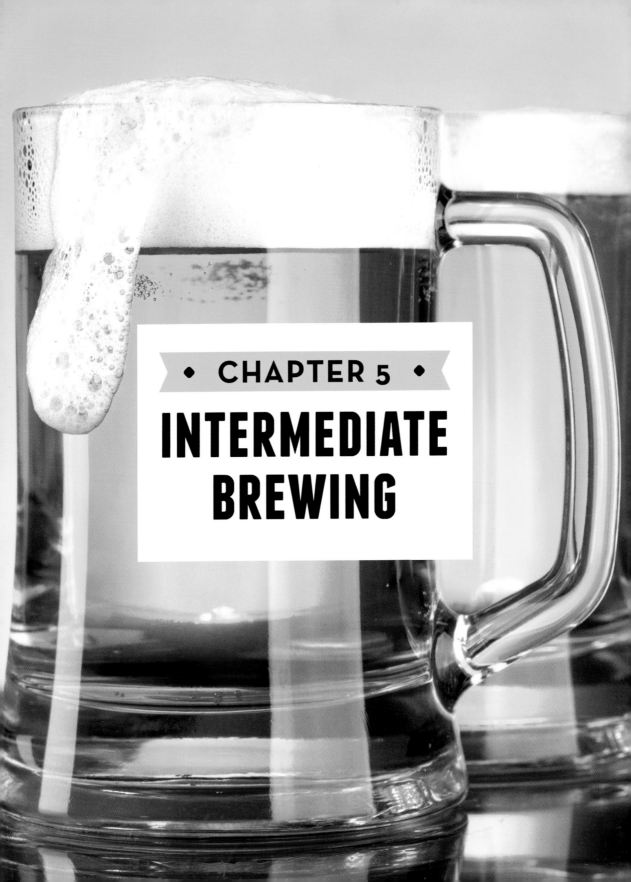

• CHAPTER 5 •

INTERMEDIATE BREWING

This chapter will introduce advanced concepts and techniques aimed at helping you produce better beer. Some terms that have been glossed over earlier will be explored in greater detail, and you will be introduced to some new procedures. This section is intended for the brewer who has reached a level of ease and comfort with novice procedures, and is ready to step up his or her knowledge and brewing system. Here you will learn how to make partial-mash homebrew, how to predict actual bitterness, how to adjust the mineral content of your brew liquor, and more.

Intermediate brewing is more demanding than extract brewing, but it's not brain surgery either. You don't need to master chemistry or memorize Latin to make a superior brew. You just need a thirst, that commonly increases among homebrewers, to learn, experiment, and have fun. The only mistake a homebrewer can make is to decide that he or she can't progress toward more complex procedures. Barring bacterial infection, all botched brew can be drunk. Furthermore, the more you brew, the better your product will become. So don't fear. Enjoy the process, learn from your mistakes, and enjoy the beer you create.

MEDITATING ON MALT

Now we'll turn our attention back to grains—using and understanding them—and we'll also look at predicting specific gravity and color.

Much to the bewilderment of contented extract brewers, some roguish, restless adventurers insist on using grains as the whole of their grist. They'll spend weeks grappling with junkyard, scrap, hammering and tinkering in the garage, constructing the internal, eternal dream of the perfect all-grain system. So often they succeed. And extract brewers who puzzle over such labor admit with leaden hearts that these alchemists have created a superior elixir.

▲ Keep thorough records of all the spices you use in your beer.

PARTIAL-MASH BREWING

What advantage do brewers who use grain have over those who use only extract? Well, for one they have greater control. Even with extracts of the highest quality, you are confined by the contents of the package. Extract brewing is real brewing, but the brewer lacks the range available to those who add grains. Partial-mash brewing is the link between the novice and the advanced brewer. By adding fermentable grains and adjuncts to your extract, you will gain the freshness and range of style and nuance enjoyed by all-grain brewers.

There are many ways you can add grain to your extract to improve your beer. Earlier, I showed you how to add specialty grains to enhance the character of your extract homebrew. Specialty grains don't require mashing. You are simply deriving color, flavor, and body from the small additions. Partial-mash brewing requires that you mash the grains prior to adding them to the brewpot. By mashing, you are converting modified starches into fermentable (and unfermentable) sugars, while taking care not to extract tannins from the husk. Besides the pride you will gain in knowing that you successfully converted starch to sugar, you will notice your homebrew take on a fresher flavor. Once you see how easy mashing can be, you may even decide to venture into the ultimate practice of professionals and advanced homebrewers: all-grain brewing.

All-grain brewers use three popular mashing procedures: single infusion, step mashing, and decoction mashing. Each method attempts to utilize two major enzymes (among others) within the malt: alpha amylase and beta amylase. Both enzymes break down long chains of carbohydrates into fermentable

▲ Alpha amylase and beta amylase in malt break down into fermentable compounds.

compounds. However, each works differently and at different temperatures. Alpha amylase breaks down compounds somewhat randomly. It may disconnect the molecules in the center of the chain creating dextrins, or near the ends, creating smaller chunks of glucose. Alpha amylase is most active at a temperature range of 150–158°F (66–70°C). Beta amylase methodically shears off glucose molecules at the ends of the long carbohydrate chains. This enzyme works at lower temperatures, with the high end being around 140°F (60°C). Both enzymes are needed to convert starches into sugars fully. By far the most simple and popular mashing method is the single-infusion mash. This simply means that the malt is added at a temperature that makes use of both enzymes. While step mashing and decoction mashing traditionally promote a more thorough starch conversion, the

well-modified malts that are available today work fine with the single-infusion method.

There are two popular techniques for single-infusion partial-mash brewing. For each method, I recommend the use of a propane gas burner and an accurate, reliable thermometer. A high-BTU burner offers much more control than any range-heating element. Metal probe thermometers work well, as they respond to temperature changes more quickly than glass mercury thermometers.

PREPARING YOUR GRAINS

Before you mash you must crush the grains. Proper crushing means you extrude and crumble the grain interior leaving the husks intact. The ideal would be that you turn the endosperm into tiny granules and leave the husk an empty sack. Commercial breweries use large, expensive roller mills to get the job done. Since you are using only a small amount of grain, you have a few less expensive options.

Many homebrew supply stores have grain crushers on the premises. If you decide to use one of these mills, make sure there is no residual material in the machine. Run it empty for half a minute while you shake the outlet tube. This should clear the mill of any debris. There are several electric and manual roller mills on the market that range in price. For a small amount of money you can pick up a Corona mill that can be adjusted to give your grains the crush they need. The mill crushes by forcing grain between two grooved plates, one of which is rotated by hand. You'll need to adjust the gap between the plates to achieve a proper crush. The plates are quickly and easily adjustable, so fiddle with them until your grain comes out right. Alternatively, accept that buying crushed grain is more efficient.

In Chapter 1, we saw how to make beer from a malt extract kit. There are two further techniques that you can use to brew beer at home. The first is partial use of grain as a source of flavor and color. The other is, as we saw at the start of Chapter 1, doing it like the pros—all-grain brewing.

▼ Vintage engraving showing a scene from 19th-century London, England. Men mixing the malt in a London brewery circa 1870.

METHOD ONE: STEEPING AND SPARGING

For the first technique, partial-mash brewing, a small amount of grain is used to give added color and flavor to the liquid extract. In addition to your regular extract brewing equipment, you'll need a large strainer, a grain-steeping bag (optional), a 2-gallon (9-liter) saucepan, and about ½ gallon (2 liters) of extra water that has been preheated to 170°F (77°C). Here is a step-by-step explanation:

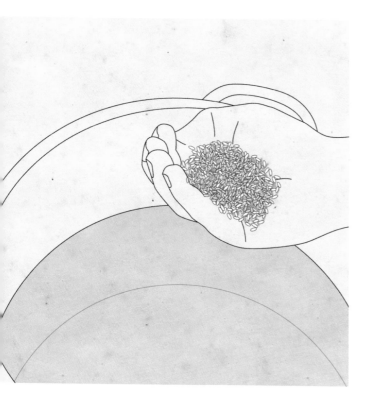

1. Heat 1/2-3/4 gallon (2-3 liters) of water in the saucepan to about 158ºF (70ºC). Add your grains (in the steeping bag or loose) and maintain a temperature range of 152-158ºF (67-70ºC). Let this mixture stand for about 45 minutes.

2. Place a large strainer over your brewpot and pour the grains and liquid into the strainer, allowing the liquid to filter into the pot.

3. Now slowly pour the ½ gallon (2¼ liters) of preheated water over the grains.

4. Remove any floating husks from the brewpot, add water, and brew as usual.

That's really all there is to mashing. By heating the water to 158°F (70°C), you are allowing both enzymes to do their thing. Maintaining the above temperature range for 45 minutes facilitates conversion. Sparging the grains with 170°F (77°C) water rinses excess sugars, while keeping tannins from the husk from dissolving.

METHOD TWO: ALL-GRAIN BREWING

The second method is more complex, but the control that you have over the recipe and the results can, for many brewers, outweigh the extra work. The process of mashing extracts the fermentable sugar from the grain, so rather than opening a can and stirring the extract into water, you are using hot water to extract the sugar from the grain. It requires the use of a 10-gallon (37-liter) mash tun (the converted picnic cooler-type works best), some transfer tubing, and a tincture of iodine.

The transfer tubing allows a smooth transfer of liquid from the bucket into the brewpot. The iodine is used to test for starch conversion. When iodine comes into contact with starch, it turns from yellow to blue or purple-black, depending on the starch concentration.

Mashing at 150–155°F (66–68°C) allows the enzymes present in the grain to convert the starch in the malt into sugar. This is a complex process, and there are many ways that you can use the mash to fine-tune the characteristics of your beer. One of the simpler and more easily detectable ones is that by mashing hotter, the wort becomes less fermentable, and produces a more full-bodied beer. Beware—excessive heat will draw tannins from the grain husks and you will denature ("kill") the enzymes, making conversion impossible.

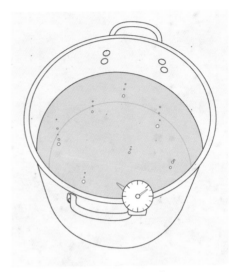

1. Heat 4½ gallons (20 liters) of water to 176°F (80°C), and run 2 gallons (9 liters) into the mash tun.

▶ Lauter bucket and sieve.

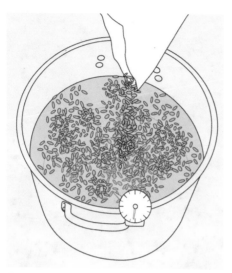

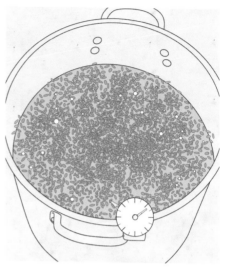

2. Monitor the temperature of the mash water as it falls, and when it reaches around 162ºF (72ºC), add 9 pounds (4 kilograms) of grain and stir.

3. Take the temperature of the mash, and add up to another ½ gallon (2 liters) of hot or cold water to achieve the desired mash temperature.

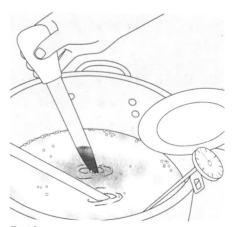

4. Stir thoroughly, put the lid on the mash tun, and maintain a temperature range of 152–158ºF (67–70ºC); in practice, this will happen if the tun is suitably insulated.

5. After 45 minutes, using a turkey baster or a ladling spoon, extract a small sample of wort from the mash, taking care not to pick up any floating grain husks.

6. *Pour this into a plate and add a few drops of iodine. If the solution turns blue or purple, there are still starches in the pot and mashing should continue.*

7. *Repeat this test periodically until there is no change in the sample. Note: do not introduce the test wort back into the mashing pot. Pour it down the sink and rinse the plate.*

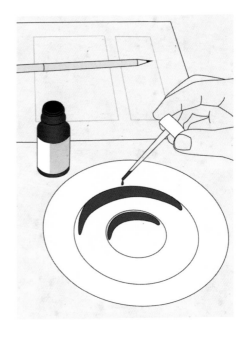

8. *When mashing is complete, draw ½ gallon (1 liter) of wort through the tap of the mash tun into a clear measuring cup. You'll probably notice that the sample is cloudy.*

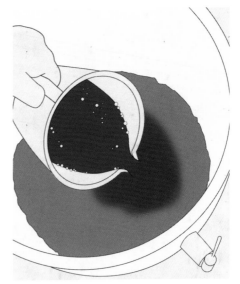

9. *Gently pour the sample back into the mash tun and repeat the process until the wort looks relatively clear.*

10. *Now connect the transfer tubing to the spigot and direct the other end into your brewpot. Slowly siphon the liquid into the pot, being very careful not to allow it to bubble or splash—oxygenating the wort at this stage can have a negative impact on the long-term stability of the beer.*

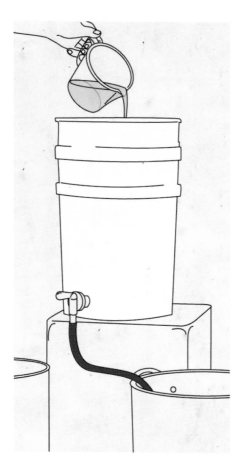

11. *As the wort runs out, slowly add water to the top of the mash tun, matching the flow out with the preheated water. Don't disturb the grain, but add water gently and evenly. Once all the liquid is collected into the brewpot, add water and brew as usual.*

By slowly running off into your brewpot and adding water to the top of the tun (which you'll remember is called sparging), you are creating a natural filter bed using the grain husks, and rinsing the sugar out of the grain.

This is very much a thumbnail sketch of how all-grain brewing works. It's a process that, once you've seen it done once, is hard to forget, and the 11 steps outlined above are a very basic template for an endless variety of recipes and techniques available.

PREDICTING GRAVITY AND COLOR

Using the Malt Profiles table (see page 198) at the back of this book, you can gain a rough estimate of the original gravity and color your malt additions will give to your homebrew. As you read this section and the sections on hop bitterness predictions and yeast, keep in mind that your primary goal is to make delicious homebrew. Don't get so bogged down in predictions and calculations that you lose sight of this objective. With that in mind, let's explore the specifics of gravity and the spectrum of colorful possibility awaiting you and your brew.

FEELING GRAVITY'S PULL

Predicting original gravity is simple but somewhat inaccurate. To calculate original gravity, you are merely multiplying the gravities proffered by the various malts, sugars, and adjuncts by the amount of each addition that will enter your pot, adding the totals, and dividing the sum by the volume of finished beer (5 gallons/23 liters, in our case). For example, say you are adding 6.6 lb (3 kg) of amber malt extract syrup and 1 lb (450 g) of crystal malt. Looking up the respective gravities in the Malt Profiles table you find that 1 lb (450 g) of the syrup yields about 1.040 per gallon of water and the crystal malt affords 1.030 per gallon. Dropping the decimals, you have 40 and 30. Your equation would look like this:

$$40 \times 6.6 = 264$$
$$30 \times 1 \quad = 30$$
$$294/5 = 58.8 \text{ or an OG of } 1.059$$

SRM/ Lovibond	Example	Beer Color	EBC
2	Pale lager		4
3	German Pilsner		6
4	Pilsner Urquell		8
6			12
8	Weissbier		16
10	Bass pale ale		20
13			26
17	Dark lager		33
20			39
24			47
29	Porter		57
35	Stout		69
40			79
>40	Imperial stout		138

▲ The imperfect brewing system means you will not get 100 percent of the potential gravity—that doesn't prevent you brewing delicious and potent beer.

This is a dicey business. First, extracts tend to offer gravity ranges rather than specific numbers. Second, crushing and mashing methods will dictate how much of the theoretical maximum of gravity you'll get from grain. No honest professionals or homebrewers will claim to get 100 percent of the potential gravity. No system is perfect.

To gauge the efficiency of your system, look up one of the recipes in this or another book. Calculate the original gravity using the formula on the left and check it against the recipe's original gravity. Divide it by the theoretical maximum and you'll get an efficiency percentage, usually around 85 percent. Now make that beer. Check your OG and divide that by the theoretical max. Now you'll have some idea about the efficiency of your system.

Keep in mind that different brands of extract may yield different original gravities. If a recipe calls for John Bull extract, for example, you may get a higher or lower yield by using another brand.

One final caveat: when you brew with a concentrated wort and dilute it, you may not get an accurate OG. Water and wort do not instantly blend into a solution. The larger the quantity of wort you can actually boil, the more accurate your reading will be.

▶ This Pilsner is about a "4" on the Lovibond scale.

APPROXIMATING COLOR

Predicting color is even more perplexing than predicting gravity. In the US, Standard Reference Method (SRM) is used to analyze beer color. The SRM scale is based on an older system called the Lovibond scale, which measured malt color. Often, you'll see Lovibond ratings on malt and grain. For practical purposes, the two scales are the same. Accurate SRM measurement requires the use of a spectrophotometer. If you do not have a spectrophotometer, you may be able to procure one by placing a second mortgage on your house. Barring this potentially relationship-breaking decision, you'll have to rely on other means.

Color in liquid is not the same as color on a solid. Pour most of a homebrew into your favorite glass and the remainder into your hydrometer. Hold the samples up to a light source. Your glass of brew will appear darker. Why? The larger volume allows less light to pass through, creating a deeper color. Next, pour the two samples into the sink. Just kidding. Drink them.

▼ Stout is a very dark beer.

SRM is simply a scale that helps define the lightness or darkness of a beer. It is in no way a substitute for the human eye. SRM does not reveal subtleties of hue, and cannot differentiate between a yellow or light-gold beer. Therefore, in addition to assigning a beer to an SRM range, brewers and beer judges often use words to convey variances that are too fine to be captured by the scale. For example, a witbier and a Pilsner have SRM ratings between 2 and 4.5. Yet, witbier is a pale, almost flat-looking yellow, while a Pilsner's yellow is effulgent. This is due to the ingredients and process involved in making the two beers. The SRM scale certainly works for beer styles with dramatically different colors. An opaque stout has an SRM rating of over 40, while a pale to golden weizen ranges between 3 and 10.

A good weekend experiment is to gather together some friends and purchase the following beer styles: wit (2–4 SRM), Pils (3–4.5 SRM), weizen (3–10 SRM), India pale ale (7–14 SRM), brown ale (14–35 SRM), porter (30–45 SRM), and dry stout (35–70 SRM). Pour the same amount of each into identical glasses. Now line them up with a light source behind them, and study the differences in color. Notice the shades of burgundy catching the edges of the porter, as the staunch stout collects all light like a silky black hole. Note the copper color of the IPA next to the deeper color of the brown ale. The spectrum of colors will offer you some perspective.

One way to approximate color is with homebrew color units (HCUs). Multiply the SRM or Lovibond rating assigned to each ingredient by how much of that malt or adjunct you use. Add the totals and divide by the volume of beer (5 gallons/23 liters). This will give you a rough estimate of final beer color.

Of course, extracts rarely give specific color ratings, and factors such as length of boil, concentration of wort, cooling rate, and fermentation conditions all obscure calculations. Still, like the formula used to estimate OG, HCUs give you some idea of color.

The best way to learn is through experience. Brew styles of different color,

keeping good records on the worksheets. Notice how different percentages of malts blend to create color. Use calculations to point you in the right direction, but rely on instinct to fine-tune your palette.

▼The intermediate brewer can create many different styles and colors of beer at home.

ENTERING THE CONE

Here's where we'll take a closer look at the role of hops in homebrewing. Hops are used to balance the sweet malt and to add flavor and aroma to your final beer. Alpha acids are responsible for the bitterness, and essential oils furnish flavor and bouquet. Let's examine these valuable hop components.

ALPHA ACIDS

Hops contain both hard resins and soft resins. Hard resins are not soluble, even with the addition of heat, and therefore contribute nothing to the bitterness of beer. Soft resins are divided into several groups, including alpha and beta acids. As we saw earlier, under normal conditions beta acids are not soluble and don't contribute much to beer. However, prolonged exposure to air oxidizes hop resins, minimizing the effects of alpha acids and amplifying the effects of beta acids. Beta acids lend a harsher, less pleasing bitterness to beer, so proper storage is important.

Alpha acids are composed of three major components: humulone, cohumulone, and adhumulone.

Researchers are still studying the specific role each of these three compounds plays in supplying bitterness. Cohumulone has been found to be the most soluble of the three, and is said to impart a harsher bitterness than humulone and adhumulone. While the concentrations of these compounds vary from harvest to harvest, higher-alpha hops tend to contain more cohumulone. For this reason, some brewers favor larger additions of lower-alpha hops to achieve bittering levels.

◀ Hops provide the alpha acids necessary for bitterness.

ALPHA-ACID UTILIZATION

Alpha Acid Units give you some idea how much bitterness is entering your wort. However, it is important to understand that only a small percentage of alpha acid remains in the wort. Only alpha acids that have gone through the chemical rearrangement known as isomerization end up in your fermenter. Even isomerized alpha acids can be lost through fermentation, filtration, and the addition of fining agents. An optimistic calculation is around 30 percent. The rest are lost in the boil.

Here are some of the variables that affect hop utilization:

1. Length of boil
2. Wort gravity
3. Hopping rate
4. Freshness of the hops
5. Vigorous fermentation
6. Hot break and cold break
7. Yeast sedimentation
8. Filtration
9. Water hardness

PREDICTING BITTERNESS: IBUS

International bittering units (IBUs) measure the amount of iso-alpha acids in beer. One IBU, or simply BU, equals one milligram per liter of iso-alpha acid in solution. You can gain a rough estimate by using a predictive formula. If AAUs tell you how much bitterness is going into your brewpot, IBU formulas predict how much will actually be utilized. Several knowledgeable brewers have created formulas and tables designed to predict IBUs. Byron Burch, Randy Mosher, Jackie Rager, and Mark Garets have all published calculation tables. I have chosen to use a formula devised by Glenn Tinseth. I like his method because it is not too complex, yet I have found it useful in my own brewing experience. The two main empirical factors he takes into account are wort gravity and boil time (the time hops spend in the boil). Using his Hop Utilization table (see page 207) and a simple formula, you can calculate how many IBUs you will attain by adding a given amount of hops with various alpha-acid percentages. Using this method, along with the Beer Style Guidelines (see page 196), you can formulate your own methods for bitterness.

▼ A sample is drawn to taste the beer in a German brewery.

HOW TINSETH'S FORMULA WORKS:

Say you are brewing a batch of your favorite homebrew that has an original gravity of 1.060. You are bittering with 2 oz (50 g) of Northern Brewer (NB) hops with an alpha acid content of 8 percent. You plan on adding 1 oz (25 g) for 60 minutes and the other for 30 minutes. How many IBUs will this yield? Here is the basic formula:

IBUs = decimal alpha acid utilization x mg/l of added alpha acids

Using Tinseth's chart, we see that the alpha acid utilization for the additions are 0.211 for the NB hops boiled for 60 minutes and 0.162 for those boiled for 30 minutes. To calculate mg/liter of added alpha acids, use the following formula:

$$\text{mg/l of added alpha acids} = \frac{\text{decimal AA rating x oz hops x 7490}}{\text{Volume of finished beer in gallons}}$$

So

$$\text{mg/l of added alpha acids} = \frac{0.08(8\% \text{ AA}) \text{ x2 (oz) x 7490}}{5 \text{ gallons}}$$

Equals: 239.68

Divide this number by half, as you are adding in stages: 119.84

Now plug this number into the IBU formula:

For the 60-minute addition: IBUs = 0.211 x 119.84, or about 26 IBUs
For the 30-minute addition: IBUs = 0.162 x 119.84, or about 19 IBUs
Adding these two numbers together, you come up with 45 IBUs

If you want to lower the number of IBUs you can either add fewer hops or use a variety with a lower alpha acid percentage. If you want to lower your IBUs by cutting your additions by, say one-quarter, you'll be adding 1½ oz (40 g) NB hops with an AA percent of 8. To find mg/l of added alpha acids, simply substitute 1½ oz (40 g) for 2 oz (50 g). Some quick calculations will give you 179.76. Divide this in half and plug these numbers into 60- and 30-minute additions: about 19 IBUs for the 60-minute additions: about 19 IBUs for the 60-minute addition and about 15 IBUs for those added at the 30-minute mark for a total of 34 IBUs. If you are using a lower-alpha-acid hop, simply apply the new percentage into the equation, keeping the amount of added hops the same (2 oz/50 g).

THE ESSENCE OF OILS

No two types of hops impart the same flavor and aroma to your beverage. There are dozens of hop varieties available to the homebrewer, and each contains a different concentration of the volatile oils that affect your brew. Cascade and Saaz are both varieties of *Humulus lupulus*, but no one can argue that they taste the same in the glass. Diverse forms of the same hop, and when and how they are introduced, will impart different characteristics. Some brewers add flavoring hops within the last few minutes of the boil. Others filter their hot wort through whole-hop beds before cooling, to pick up aromas and flavors. A different bouquet is achieved by introducing pellet, plug, or whole hops into your secondary fermenter.

What makes for such a wide range of scent and taste? All plants contain oils. Hop researchers have identified 22 essential oil components that influence the flavor and aroma of beer. These are subdivided into three groups: humulene and caryophylene oxidation products; floral–estery compounds; and citrus–piny compounds. These appear, in varying proportions, in the prized aroma hops that homebrewers use to crown their beer.

FLEECING THE FLEETING OILS

Since these oils are volatile, they tend to dissipate quickly. Poorly stored hops, or hops that have endured a prolonged boil, will contribute little flavor and aroma to the finished product. Follow the storage recommendations for hops to preserve the delicate oils. Constrain any finishing hop additions to the final 20 minutes of the total boil. The longer you leave them in, the less good they'll do. Finally, proper brewing procedure will discourage the introduction of oxygen at the wrong time. Oxidation affects many compounds in your wort and beer, and hop oils are no exception. There are many detailed studies of this interaction available online.

The Internet is a hugely valuable resource for the home brewer. Whether looking for a forum, a website, or a piece of software to help you calculate and archive your recipes, a little judicious searching will yield a whole heap of useful results.

▲ Dark porter beer in a glass.

ATTENUATION, PLEASE: ANOTHER LOOK AT YEAST

Even the most fanatical homebrewer must eventually step away from the fermenter and let the yeast go to work. Fermentation, aging, and conditioning normally work best without human intervention, save prayers, incantations, and good luck rituals. Homebrewers merely set fermentation into motion. After this, we are spectators. However, not all fermentation goes as planned. Sometimes the yeast seems to take forever to begin working. Other times, fermentation rolls on ceaselessly in a neverending plop of bubbles through the airlock. You may see a batch that starts fermenting strongly and swiftly, then suddenly stops. Such symptoms may be traced to bacterial infection, underpitching, or improper fermentation problems. Conversely, while overpitching may not be the most cost-effective way to start fermentation, it is unlikely that it will do any harm.

ALWAYS PITCH ENOUGH YEAST

At the height of fermentation, there are roughly 50 million yeast cells per milliliter of wort. After this, the yeast cells start to drop from suspension into a bed of sediment and become dormant.

The desired pitching rate for the purposes of homebrewing is in the range of five to ten million cells per milliliter of wort for ales and even more for lagers. Underpitching puts a strain on yeast that might result in long lag times (the quiet period between pitching and apparent fermentation), protracted fermentation times, and stuck fermentation. If you want to know how thoroughly your yeast strain is attenuating in the primary you can use the following formula:

AAP (Apparent Attenuation Percentage) = [(original gravity—final gravity)/original gravity] x 100

For example, if the original gravity of your wort is 1.060 and the final gravity of the beer is 1.020, the equation would look like this (drop the decimals on the gravity readings):

$$AAP = \frac{(60-20)}{60} = 0.666 \times 100 = 67\% \text{ apparent attenuation}$$

If your readings fall below this range, your yeast is not fully attenuating. This may well be the result of pitching too little yeast. Keep in mind that lager yeast will ferment a broader range of wort sugars and typically has a higher attenuation percentage. You can increase the amount of yeast that goes into the fermenter by making a yeast starter.

PREPARING A YEAST STARTER: AVOID CULTURE SHOCK

Yeast starters work by gradually introducing yeast to larger and larger volumes of wort. Once the liquid pack is prepared, the yeast cells thrive within a small amount of sterile wort. However, the yeast colony is still young and vulnerable. A yeast starter is a slightly larger volume of sanitary wort that allows the yeast to strengthen and multiply before taking the 5-gallon (23-liter) plunge. Considering it takes a day or two for a liquid packet to "strengthen" and a day extra for the starter to become viable, plan these procedures 2 to 3 days before you brew.

To make a yeast starter:

1-gallon (4.5-liter) bottle that will accept a rubber stopper and airlock (empty "growlers," containers brewpubs use to sell draft beer, work well)

A drilled rubber stopper and airlock

1 quart (1 liter) of water

3 oz (75 g) of dried malt extract

One packet of liquid yeast

Continues overleaf...

◀ A yeast starter takes at least a day to become viable.

1. *Sanitize the bottle and cap it off with a piece of aluminum foil. Also, sanitize the rubber stopper and airlock. In a shallow pan boil the DME in the water for 10 minutes.*

2. *Cool the wort by placing the covered pan in ice water. Swab the mouth of the bottle with a ball of cotton soaked in alcohol.*

3. *Flame it with a lighter.*

4. *Pour in the wort.*

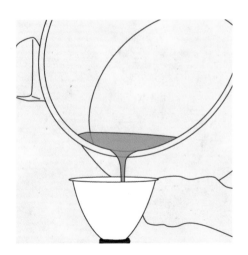

5. *Now add the yeast.*

6. *Seal the bottle with an airlock and stopper.*

7. *Aerate the bottle by agitating it for several minutes. Maintain temperatures between 65–75ºF (18–24ºC). Once active fermentation is apparent (12 hours or more) your starter is ready to pitch into the fermenter.*

8. *Remove the airlock and stopper, swab and flame any surfaces the starter may make contact with, and pour into the wort.*

CHAPTER 5: INTERMEDIATE BREWING

ALE CREATURES GREAT AND SMALL (AND EVEN LAGER!)

If yeast merely converted malt sugars into alcohol and CO_2, the brewing world would have less variety to offer. Indeed, many of the by-products of fermentation help define the distinct characteristics of certain beer styles. On the other hand, some by-products are less desirable, and can (sometimes literally) cause headaches. Here are some organic compounds created during fermentation.

Aldehydes This group of acids causes a range of flavors, from a green-apple aroma to a flat flavor of "wet cardboard."

Esters This class of compounds produces fruity aromas. Some ales, such as German weizen, depend on some esters to give wheat beer its trademark banana aroma. Lager yeast produces far fewer esters than ale yeast.

Diacetyl Responsible for buttery or butterscotch aromas, diacetyl is more characteristic of ales than lagers. While its presence can be indicative of poor technique, a couple of styles require a certain diacetyl flavor.

Fusel alcohols Ethyl alcohol defines the potency of beer, and is the desired product of fermentation. However, yeast also produces more complex alcohol compounds that can give beer a harsh bite and even cause slight headaches. Fusel alcohol is a naturally occurring compound that is generally produced early in fermentation. Some homebrewers affix "blow-off" tubing on their primary fermenters in an attempt to expel this unpleasant compound.

Organic acids Contaminated wort can result in high levels of these "goaty-flavored" substances.

Again, different strains of yeast ferment wort in different ways. By keeping your equipment sanitary, cooling your wort quickly, and choosing good-quality yeast suited to your targeted style, you'll easily control the perceptible levels of these and other by-products. If you feel you've met all of the above requirements and still make beer that is unsatisfactory, see "Troubleshooting" on pages 208–210.

Clean, healthy yeast should produce great homebrew. The proliferation of quality liquid yeast strains has improved the quality and range of homebrew tremendously. There are yeast strains available for every type of beer, from the simplest ale to the most complex lambic. The key to good results is providing your yeast population with the right conditions, including temperature, handling, and propagation. Some high-gravity worts benefit from adding a yeast starter. This is not hard to do—it just requires a little extra time and cheap equipment. Never underestimate the role of yeast. Choosing a quality liquid strain that suits your particular style is as crucial as every other aspect of homebrewing.

138

WATER EVERYWHERE, BUT WHAT TO DRINK?

Earlier I explained that, for the extract brewer, the most important qualities of brew water are potability and taste. Two additional characteristics that are important in all-grain brewing are pH level and ion content. The pH level refers to the acidic or alkaline nature of a liquid. The pH scale ranges from 1 (strongly acidic) to 14 (strongly alkaline) with 7 being neutral. Most water supplies hover around 7, though this can and does change.

Ions are electrically charged particles that influence chemical reactions in brewing and affect beer flavor. Ions may be one atom or a group that attach to similar charges in water. All natural water contains ions. The ionic content of water and the relationship ions have with the brewing process is complex, so I'm not going to explore the subject in detail here. It is not necessary to totally understand water chemistry to make great beer. However, if you are mashing a portion of your fermentables, it does help to understand the basics.

You may be thinking: "If beer making began as a natural process, why do we need to bother with water chemistry?" Certain ions help to lower the pH of mash water, activating key enzymes within malt. Other ions increase the solvency of brew liquor, letting it retain qualities from malt and hops. Ions—like copper and magnesium—in trace amounts are a vital nutrient for yeast.

PH AND BREWING

The partial mash brewer usually adds grains to preheated water (150–158°F/66–70°C) for 45 minutes to an hour. This "single infusion" mash allows two major enzymes—alpha amylase, and to a lesser extent, beta amylase—to become active and convert long carbohydrate chains into maltose, glucose, and other fermentable sugars. Just as certain

▲ Mineral adding must be very precise.

temperatures are needed to activate and sustain enzyme activity, so too is a specific pH range. A mildly acidic mash (5.2–5.8) must be maintained for these enzymes to do their thing.

Luckily, many malts contain natural acidic phosphates which lower the pH in the brewpot to proper levels. A highly alkaline water supply, however, may not come down to proper pH range by the mere addition of malt. Water that is high in bicarbonates (HCO_3-1) may require treatment before use.

▲ Keeping a constant eye on pH is important in brewing.

pH
You can measure pH using either paper test strips or a digital device. Test strips are cheaper but less accurate. These are dipped into a cool sample of liquid and held against a color chart to read pH. Digital meters can be dipped directly into the mash for a fast readout.

IONS AND WATER

Expressed chemically, water is simply composed of two hydrogen atoms bound to a single oxygen atom. Like many compounds, water has a slight electrical charge: a partial positive from the hydrogen and a partial negative from the oxygen. These charges "seek" other molecules and atoms with similar charges to form bonds. Hence, table salt (Na+Cl) will dissolve in water because the positive sodium will bond with hydrogen and the negative chloride ion will bond with oxygen. Ions in water help to dissolve compounds that otherwise would fall out of solution. Calcium, for example, helps to dissolve resins and oils in hops. Distilled or "deionized" water would not be able to dissolve such compounds.

Certain ions help to adjust the pH of water. Calcium and magnesium both help to make brew water more acidic. Brewers often add gypsum (calcium sulfate), calcium carbonate, Epsom salts (magnesium sulfate), or other salts to lower mash pH.

Some ions have no chemical effect in brewing, but do contribute flavor. Small amounts of sodium give beer a smooth, rounded flavor. Sulfates paired with high levels of hop resins will give beer a harsh, bitter taste. Such effects must be considered when adding salts.

Copper, magnesium, and zinc are vital yeast nutrients at trace levels. Since most water contains small amounts of these, you shouldn't try to add any more. All three are detrimental to your beer if present in excess.

TEMPORARY AND PERMANENT HARDNESS

Brewers speak of "temporary hardness" to describe water that is high in bicarbonates. However, water high in calcium and magnesium tends to be acidic, while water with excess bicarbonates is usually alkaline. You want water to be slightly acidic to promote starch conversion during the mash. Therefore, you won't want excessive levels of bicarbonate in your brew water. Unlike other ions, bicarbonates can be removed from your brew water by boiling and pouring the water off the precipitated minerals. If there are chalky deposits ringing the basins in your home, you can assume that your water has a high bicarbonate content.

MEASURING THE MINERALS

Ions are expressed in parts per million (ppm). This measurement is the same as the more easily applied milligrams per liter (mg/l). If you want to know the ionic content of your municipal supply, you can get a free analysis from your water company on the following components:

Calcium Used to lower mash pH and accentuate hop flavors in beer. Look for levels of at least 50 ppm, but not over 100 ppm. An exception to this rule is the hard water of Burton upon Trent in the British Midlands, which is used for brewing pale and India pale ales. There is as much as 295 ppm of calcium in these waters.

Carbonate/bicarbonate So-called "temporary hardness," this is often expressed as the total alkalinity of water. Keep levels under 50 ppm when brewing pale beers and 250 ppm when brewing dark beers.

Chloride Low levels accentuate malt and hops characteristics. Higher levels give beer a rounded, smooth flavor. Look for levels below 100 ppm.

Copper Trace levels are a nutrient for yeast. Appreciable levels can be toxic to yeast.

Iron Excessive amounts of iron will give your water, and hence your beer, a metallic, "bloodlike" taste. Anything above a trace is undesirable.

Magnesium Small amounts accentuate beer flavor, lower pH, and are a nutrient for yeast. At levels above 30 ppm, it can cause harsh flavors. At 50–100 ppm it can give beer a smooth, pleasant taste.

Sulfate Normally in the range of 10 ppm for Pilsners to 70 ppm for ales.

Zinc Anything above a trace in water to be used for brewing is undesirable.

▶ Magnesium may be needed in trace amounts.

ADJUSTING ION CONTENT

Adjusting the mineral content of water to duplicate a famous style of beer, bring out a flavor, or to change pH can be tricky. Don't add salts until you understand the chemistry. Common brewing salts include: gypsum (calcium sulfate); calcium carbonate; Epsom salts (magnesium sulfate); calcium chloride; non-iodized table salt (sodium chloride).

CONDITIONING YOUR BREW

Once your ale has finished fermenting, or your high-gravity ale or lager has matured, you may either bottle or keg. At this point your beer is beer, sans bubbles. To give your homebrew this final touch, you must carbonate it. The two methods of carbonation are bottle or keg conditioning and forced carbonation. The former simply means that you add 5 oz (150 g) corn sugar (glucose) or 10 oz (300 g) DME (mainly maltose) to reactivate yeast suspended in your 5-gallon (23-liter) batch of brew. Even though the yeast may be done fermenting the compounds in the malt, adding sugar will supply enough extra food for one last meal. This will cause the yeast to produce carbon dioxide, just the stuff you need to give your homebrew zing. By capping your bottles or securing the lid on your keg, the evolving gas will have nowhere to go except back into the beer.

Give your primed and sealed brew two weeks to achieve desirable carbonation. Remember, if you are using bottles make sure they are brown, pop-top, and sturdy. Quite a bit of CO_2 is created during bottle conditioning so be sure your bottles can take the pressure. Popular types of bottles include 12 oz (350 g), 22 oz (650 g), and 6 oz (175 g) "nip" bottles for high-potency homebrew. You can bottle in style and ease using bottles with a ceramic or plastic swing top. These are equipped with replaceable rubber washers that form a tight seal.

Forced carbonation requires the use of a CO_2 tank and regulator, and either a counterflow bottle filler (for bottling) or a soda keg with proper fittings. Forced bottle carbonation is a slow process that is far beyond my patience. Force-carbonating a keg, however, is easy and vivifying. Your brew will be carbonated in a few days evenly and consistently.

BOTTLING

Most homebrewers bottle their beer. The reason for this is usually economics. Bottling requires little extra equipment, while kegging demands such pricey additions as a spare refrigerator, a keg and fittings, and a CO_2 tank and pressure regulator. All you need to bottle is some corn sugar, a short length of clear tubing, a bottle filler, a bottle capper, some caps, and, of course, bottles.

There are some advantages to bottling your beer. The first is portability. Bottles can be brought to parties, packed in picnic coolers, and given as gifts. If you come up with a particularly good recipe, bottles can be easily sent to competitions for evaluation. The main drawback is the time and effort it requires. However, there are some steps that you can take that will cut down on the time and effort you spend bottling.

▼ If you rinse bottles as soon as you've poured out the beer, it will save you scrubbing out hard sediment later.

WASH YOUR BOTTLES AFTER EACH USE

This sounds tedious, but a quick wash will save you a lot of future hassle. If you have a bottle washer, connect it to your sink before a tasting session. Decant your brew into your favorite glass and—with one eye on the creamy head and the other on the faucet—give your bottle a healthy blast of water. This will rid your bottle of the yeast sediment that would otherwise harden if left unattended.

SANITIZE EN MASSE

Properly cleaned bottles can be stored in a new plastic trashcan filled with cold water and a little sanitizing solution. When it comes time to bottle, merely pluck the bottles from the bin, give them a few rinses with hot water, and they are ready for use. Be sure to read about the details of your sanitizer, as some degrade more quickly than others leaving soaking bottles a risk of contamination. You can even store sanitized bottles dry, by placing a piece of aluminum foil over the lip and placing them in a dry closet. If you choose to soak, try to find bottles without labels. You can either meticulously scrape the labels off used bottles or buy them bare at many homebrew supply stores. If you are storing your sanitizing container outside, be sure to cover it and mark it "NOT TRASH."

▲ The bottle washer is a useful addition to your brewing equipment.

◀ A quick rinse with a bottle washer right after you pour your beer will save time.

BOTTLE 1-2-3

Some people may tell you to spoon a little corn sugar into each bottle and then fill them with the beer. Ignore these people. For expedience and efficiency, you can't beat the old bottling bucket and solution of corn sugar. Many homebrew stores sell 5-gallon (23-liter) plastic fermenters intended to hold about 3½ gallons (16 liters) of fermenting brew. These make perfect bottling buckets. Boil half a pint of water and ¾ cup (5 oz/150 g) corn sugar in a small saucepan or Pyrex glass container. Cover and let the mixture cool. Meanwhile, siphon your beer into the bottling bucket. Remember, splashing introduces air, which contains oxygen, which hastens the deterioration of your beer. Once the bucket is full, gently pour in the corn sugar mixture and stir using a sanitized, food-grade, plastic or stainless-steel spoon. Cover the bottling bucket. Connect a bottle filler to some tubing, and the tubing to the spigot on the bucket (all of which have been sanitized, of course). Soak your bottle caps in a dilute bleach–water solution for about 20 minutes.

Now, line your bottles up and begin filling. Fill to the rim and pull out the bottle filler. This should leave a little desirable space around the neck. Place a cap over the top and move onto the next bottle. When all bottles are filled, crimp the caps and mark them for identification. Store your bottles in the same dark, quiet place you stored your fermenter. Most ale will be ready to drink within two weeks.

▶ **Use bottles with swing tops for ease of use.**

145

▲ Always store your bottles upright.

SOOTHING THE SAVAGE YEAST

Any unfiltered beer will have some yeast left in suspension. This is normal. If you find that the flavor of your beer is dominated by a yeasty taste, there are a few steps you can take. First, try a period of cold-conditioning. If this doesn't work, try adding a fining agent like gelatin or isinglass before you bottle. This will help drop the yeast out of suspension. There will still be enough to facilitate carbonation, but the rest will be culled to a level better suiting your taste. Finally, always store your bottles upright, and don't shake or handle them roughly. You want to keep the sediment at the bottom of the bottle, away from your beer. When you pour a glass, stop just before the sediment reaches the lip of the bottle. Now, go to the faucet and rinse.

KEGGING

As we saw earlier, there are a number of clever devices that allow you to keg a small volume of beer. By far the most convenient, reliable, and enduring is the employment of a used 5-gallon (23-liter) soda keg. These are designed to store soft-drink syrup, which is then mixed with water and carbon dioxide. These kegs are being phased out in favor of plastic bags set inside cardboard boxes. Metal canisters can be bought used, and rigged to hold and dispense beer. Soda kegs have the added benefits of allowing quick-force carbonation, and doubling as a lagering vessel.

Depending on where you live and what equipment your local homebrew supply store stocks, you will come across various devices designed to hold your beer. Some stores sell the Party Pig®, a handy, inexpensive vessel built to hold a portion of your brew. You may also find access to small barrel-shaped kegs that use seltzer cartridges to maintain carbonation and dispense homebrew. There are a number of options on the market. The girth of your wallet may dictate which system you decide to choose.

Inevitably, every homebrewer considers kegging as an alternative to bottling. Kegging takes less time, gives you the option to force-carbonate, and holds a certain appeal that can be best described as just being "cool." There's something about bellying up to your own bar, grabbing the wooden tap handle, and pouring a pint of your latest batch of brew.

The key to successful kegging is maintenance of your equipment. Most used soda kegs have spent years squirting out soft-drink syrup, so the parts will need cleaning and/or replacing. The following parts need to be inspected: inlet and outlet valves and rubber O-rings, the rubber gasket around the lid, the liquid and gas dip tubes and O-rings, and the interior of

▶ A CO$_2$ tank and pressure regulator with appropriate gauges.

▼ Hook up the gas line to the keg to force-carbonate your homebrew.

the keg. New parts are easy to find, whether at your local store or through mail-order companies. Old parts or broken O-rings will cause leaks, making it impossible to properly carbonate your beer, keep oxygen out, and maintain pressure.

For all practical purposes, consider your keg as one big bottle. If you plan to carbonate your beer using corn sugar or DME, follow the instructions for bottling, but use about a third less priming agent. When the keg is filled, secure the lid and add some CO$_2$ pressure. Listen for leaks. If you hear any hissing, release the pressure and readjust the lid. Once you are sure of a proper seal, apply a small amount of CO$_2$ pressure and pull the purge pin to allow air to escape. This will be replaced by the incoming CO$_2$ pressure and pull the purge pin to allow air to escape and discouraging oxidation. Store your brew at appropriate temperatures for a couple of weeks.

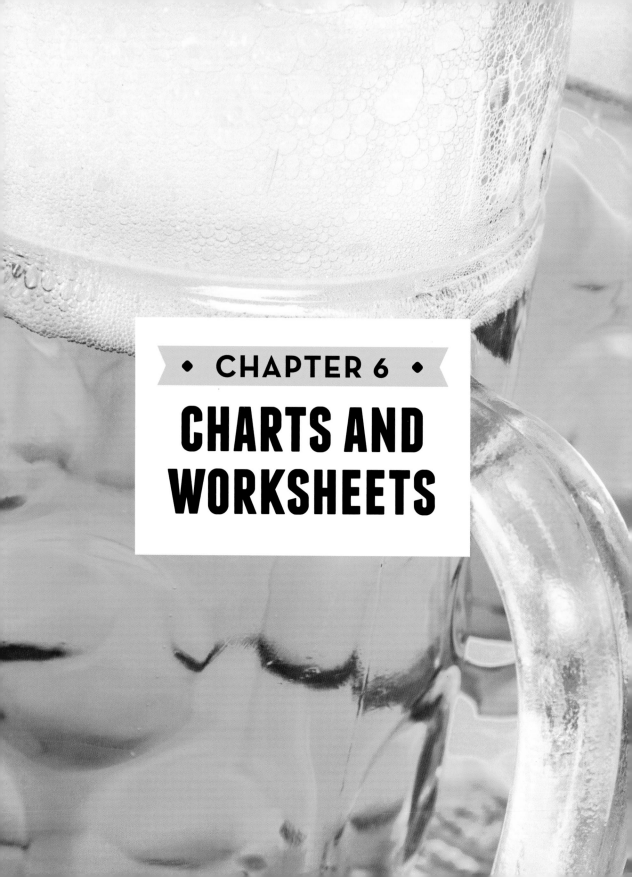

CHAPTER 6

CHARTS AND WORKSHEETS

The intermediate worksheets are designed to help you make great homebrew! Using these aids in conjunction with other information in this book, you will gain a better understanding of how each homebrew recipe ingredient affects your beer; organize all necessary recipe and procedural information in one accessible area (no frantic mid-brew page flipping); evaluate your efforts; and keep all those great batch sessions filed for later reference. As your homebrew knowledge increases, you can even create your own recipes designed to your personal taste specifications.

The worksheets are divided into four sections:

Homebrew Recipe/Worksheet
Homebrew Flowchart: Hot Side
Homebrew Flowchart: Cold Side
Homebrew Results/Journal

Each of these sections will be filled out, to some extent, before you start to brew. Doing this will constrain all the information you need to just a few pages, freeing you to concentrate on brewing your excellent beer! You'll see how to use each of these four sections in a minute, but first let's take a quick look at each.

HOMEBREW CHARTS AND WORKSHEETS

HOMEBREW RECIPE/WORKSHEET

This section is subdivided into five parts: Basic Information; Homebrew Recipe; Ingredient Characteristics Breakdown; Target Homebrew Characteristics; and Equipment/Procedural Notes.

Basic information is just that: name of beer, volume brewed, style, and so on.

In the Homebrew Recipe space, you'll enter the recipe of the beer you're going to brew, whether from this book or another.

The Ingredient Characteristics Breakdown table is designed for the homebrewer who wishes to understand how each ingredient affects the characteristics of his or her final brew. By listing all of the added malt, hops, yeast, etc., you can estimate how each contributes its unique quality to the given style of beer. Use the Ingredient Profile tables (see pages 198–206) to obtain the necessary information or, for more current statistics, use the specifications often supplied on the packaging of your malt, hops, and yeast. Once you have entered this data, use the Calculations Tables to obtain utilization estimates. While these are admittedly tentative predictions,

comparing your goals with your outcome will give you some idea about the efficiency of your system, allowing for adjustments in procedure and experimentation with different equipment and ingredients.

Imagine exploring a dark cave and, once deep inside its winding labyrinth, you suddenly realize you forgot to tie a lead rope at the entrance. You'd be lost! Wise spelunkers checklist all of their tools before taking the plunge, and as a brewer you should list all of your tools in the Equipment Procedural Notes section. Making sure all the equipment you need is sanitized and ready for use—this will save time and needless worry. The only thing you should be rushing for mid-brew is another glass of your latest homebrew. Also, variations in equipment can have an effect on the efficiency of your system. Recording the tools of your trade will serve as reason and reminder to step up the quality of your equipment.

In the Procedural column you can transfer the recipe instructions or, if you're brewing an original, you can outline your own game plan.

HOMEBREW FLOWCHART: HOT SIDE/COLD SIDE

You'll be filling out most parts of these two tables before you start brewing. Space is allotted for you to enter ingredients used and when you'll be adding them. This serves as a procedural flowchart. All that will be left for you to do while brewing is to check off each step as it is completed, and record any observations and/or incidentals as necessary. This is where it all happens and these charts will guide you through the whole process, from boil to bottle.

HOMEBREW RESULTS/JOURNAL

This section allows you to compare your results with your goals. Is your IPA properly bitter? Did you hit the right color on that last Pilsner? By comparing your results with your predictions, you'll gain an understanding of the effectiveness of your system and, perhaps, a newfound respect for all the complex variables involved in the creation of homebrew.

In the Notes area, you can offer possible reasons for why your beer hit or missed your target and plan changes in equipment and procedure for future batches. Of course, your primary concern should be whether or not your brew is tasty and drinkable. Don't let missed theoretical targets discourage you. Even the masters admit that predictions are difficult.

First enjoy what you've made, then consider what might be done to come closer to the mark next time around. Remember that you are the artist and your palette is as unique as your palate.

FILLING OUT HOMEBREW RECIPE WORKSHEETS

The easiest way to learn how to use these worksheets is by example. So let's fill one out together. Note: I've completed the worksheets as if the batch had already been brewed, to fully illustrate how each section works. Say you're working with the following 5-gallon (23-liter) recipe:

THEO'S THEORETICAL ALE
OG: 1.016 FG: 1.014 HCU: 19 IBUs: 52 Boil Time: 1 hour

8 oz (225 g) crystal malt

1 lb (450 g) pale malt

½ tsp gypsum

3⅓ lb (1.5 kg) amber malt extract

3⅓ lb (1.5 kg) light malt extract

2 oz (50 g) Northern Brewer hops

1 tsp Irish moss

1½ oz (40 g) Cascade hops

1 package Wyeast 1056 American ale yeast

5 oz (150 g) corn sugar (for priming)

METHOD

Heat 3–4 gallons (14–18 liters) water to 155°F (68°C). Add crystal and pale malts and steep 30–35 minutes, maintaining temperature. Scoop out grains and sparge with 165°F (74°C) water. Remove pot from heat; add gypsum and malt extracts. When you are sure that all extract is dissolved, return pot to heat and boil. Add 1 oz (25 g) Northern Brewer hops. Stir and watch for boil-overs. After 30 minutes, add remaining Northern Brewer hops. After 10 minutes, add Irish moss. Add 1 oz (25 g) Cascade hops during last 5 minutes of boil.

Cool wort to about 75°F (24°C) and siphon or strain into primary fermenter. Add cold water to bring wort up to 5-gallon (23-liter) mark. Pitch yeast at 65–70°F (18–21°C). Ferment at 65°F (18°C) for 4–7 days or until apparent fermentation has ceased.

Rack to secondary and add remaining ½ oz (12 g) Cascade hops. Store as before for two weeks. Prime with corn sugar and bottle or keg. Let beer carbonate and further age for one to two weeks.

FIRST ENTER YOUR BASIC INFORMATION:

Name of beer: Theo's Theoretical Ale

Date brewed: 1/24/11

Description: amber, med. body, hoppy ale

Vol. Brewed: 5 gallons (23 liters)

Style: IPA

Time: preboil/boil: 30–35 min/60 min

Next, transfer the recipe to the Homebrew Recipe table. To avoid being redundant and possibly insulting to your intelligence, I've omitted this step. I will, however, suggest that you include the forms of ingredients you'll be using (e.g. pellet hops as opposed to whole hops) as these may have some effect on how they are utilized in the brewpot and fermenter. Using the tables from pages 196–210, fill out the characteristics of each ingredient, as follows:

INGREDIENT CHARACTERISTICS BREAKDOWN

Key:
G = Gravity
L = Degrees Lovibond
% = AA%
TIME = Time spent in boil
U = Decimal utilization
ATTN% = Attenuation

Malt/ ADJ	lb	g	l	HOPS	oz	%	TIME	U	M/C	YEAST	ATTN %
Crystal	0.5	25	40	NB	1	11	60 mins	25	Gyp	W1056	73–77
Pale 2 Row	1	30	4	NB	1	11	30 mins	10	IrM		
AbME	3.3	35	50	Casc	1	5	5 mins	0			
LiME	3.3	30	5	Casc	0.5	5	Dry	0			

Note that pounds of malt and ounces of hops should be entered as decimals, gravity as a whole number (25 as opposed to 1.025), and that hops should be itemized according to the total time spent in the boil.

Using the calculations tables on pages 196–210, you can now make final predictions based on the information entered in the above table. Depending on the amount of procedural factors you wish to take into account, your calculations can be as simple or as complex as you desire.

TARGET HOMEBREW CHARACTERISTICS

OG: 1.056
FG: 1.014
HCU: 19
IBU: 52
Other: Clearly hoppy!

As we saw earlier, your predictions take into account some, but not all, of the factors involved in the transition of characteristics from ingredient to brew. The quality of your homebrew equipment can affect your procedure and the accuracy of your results.

For example, the addition of an immersion wort chiller to your system decreases the time it takes to cool. Any excessive time the wort spends between 140°F and 80°F (60°C and 27°C) allows wild yeast and bacteria to develop. This can be detrimental to all aspects of your beer. Make a note of your cooling method and consider upgrading if you're not getting the desired results.

Now enter ingredients and procedural information into the flowcharts:

EQUIPMENT/PROCEDURAL NOTES

Equipment/Procedural Notes	
6¾-gallon (30-liter) plastic fermenter (for primary)	All steps fit into flowcharts
5-gallon (23-liter) glass carboy (for aging)	
5-gallon (23-liter) brewpot	
Triple-scale hydrometer	
Floating thermometer	
Bleach (as sanitizer)	
Bottle washer (just bought it!)	
Muslin and grain bags (for grains and hops)	
Plastic tubing (for transfers and cooling siphon)	
Measuring cup and spoons	
1 gallon (4½ liters) water for sparging	
Spray bottle	
Heat source: electric hob	Cooling method: single-basin system

While the purpose of the flowcharts is to organize the recipe instructions in a chronological format, there are sometimes steps that cannot be readily entered into the flowcharts. You should highlight any such steps in the Procedural Notes section.

HOMEBREW FLOWCHART: HOT SIDE PREBOIL

I Grains Crystal malt Pale malt		II Malt extracts Amber malt extract Light malt extract		III Adjuncts None		IV Brew salts Gypsum	
1. Time added: at 155°F (68°C)	X	1. Time added: After 1 remove and sparge the grains	X	1. Time added:		1. Time added: Along with the extracts	
Temp added: Same as above	X		X	2. Time added:		Amount added: ½ tsp	X
2. Time removed: After 30–35 mins	X					2. Time added:	
Temp removed: Same as above	X					Amount added:	
Notes		Notes		Notes		Notes	
It's pretty tough to regulate temp on an electric hob. Gotta think about getting a gas burner.		Glad I warmed the extracts before trying to pour them in. That's some thick syrup!				No problems here. Hopefully this will lower the pH of my water so that more bitterness can be extracted from my hops.	

BOIL

V Boiling hops 1 oz (25 g) Northern Brewer 1 oz (25 g) Northern Brewer			VI Clarifiers Irish moss			VII Finishing hops		
1. Time(s)	Amount(s)		1. Time(s)	Amount(s)		1. Time(s)	Amount(s)	
60 mins	1 oz (25 g)	X	20 mins	1 tsp	X	5 mins	1 oz (25 g)	X
30 mins	1 oz (25 g)	X				Dry	½ oz (12 g)	X
Notes			Notes			Notes		
As soon as I added those first hops, the pot started foaming up. Luckily I had that spray bottle to avoid a boil-over.			Stirred it in and let it do its thing.			I love the smell of these hops. Maybe next time I'll put them in loose. It might help release more of those great oils.		

Note that when you enter the times you're adding the ingredients, you should do so in relation to the total time of the boil. Here, the first additions of the Northern Brewer hops are dropped at the beginning of the boil, or the 60-minute mark. The next ounce of Northern Brewer hops is added at the 30-minute mark. This means they will spend 30 minutes in the boil. The ounce of Cascade hops is introduced 55 minutes into the 60-minute boil, so enter 5 minutes as the total time spent in the wort. Working with a timer that counts down from 60 minutes, you simply add these ingredients when the corresponding times are reached.

HOMEBREW FLOWCHART: COLD SIDE

COOLING/PITCHING

VIII Cooling	IX Pitching yeast
1. Time wort removed from heat: 12.35 pm	1. Temp yeast pitched: 70ºF (21ºC)
2. Took how long to cool? 2 hours!	2. Amount pitched: 1 packet
Notes	Notes
Man, that took a long time to cool. I need to find a way to get this stuff down to pitching temp more quickly!	Made sure I sanitized and rinsed the mouth of the packet before I put in the wort. Also, I gently stirred it in with a sanitized plastic spoon. The transfer went pretty well. Only lost a little beer when the hose slipped out of the fermenter.

Here you want to record the specific time that the wort is removed from the heat, so you can time duration between near-boiling and pitching temperature.

FERMENTING/AGING

X Primary fermentation	XI Aging
1. Vessel: 6¾-gallon (30-liter) plastic fermenter	1. Date racked: 01/29/2018
2. Ambient temp: About 75ºF (24ºC)	
3. Date/time started fermenting: 10.30 pm, 1/24/2018	3. Dry hops: cascade Form: pellets Amount: ½ oz (12 g)
4. Date fermentation ceased: 1/29/2011	4. Ambient temp: About 75ºF (24ºC)
Notes	Notes
Pretty vigorous fermentation! Kept the wort cool by draping a wet T-shirt over it.	Decided to dry-hop loose and siphon the beer off later. There was a little splashing during transfer, but not too much. The beer already smells good!

PRIMING/BOTTLING

XII Priming/Bottling				
1. Priming agent: Corn sugar	Amount: 5 oz (150 g)	2. Bottled X	Kegged	Other
3. Ambient storage temp: 75ºF (24ºC)		Stored how long? Tried the first after a week. Let the rest age for the full two weeks.		
Notes				
Let age for two weeks in secondary. Wow, the beer really cleared up and actually darkened a little by the time it was ready to bottle. Primed with corn sugar, stirring it in with a sanitized plastic spoon. Bottling was crazy! I was trying to watch the siphon intake at the carboy and the filling of each bottle at the same time. The only way I could stop the flow of beer was by pinching the end of the siphon tube. What a mess! I need to get one of those plastic bottle fillers and maybe even a plastic racking cane. Maybe I'll get a bottling bucket and siphon into that first. When all was through, I had lost about 16 oz of precious brew to spillage. The capper worked great and was actually kinda fun!				

HOMEBREW RESULTS/JOURNAL

RESULTS

Predicted OG: 1.056	Actual OG: 1.052	Predicted FG: 1.014	Actual FG: 1.014	Alcohol:
Calculated IBU: 57		Perceived bitterness: Nice bitterness and wonderful floral aroma		
Calculated HCU: 19		Resultant color: Deep amber color, looks great through the light		
Desired aroma/flavor from hops: That distinctive citrusy Cascade quality		Perceived aroma/flavor: Wasn't let down, but I may dry-hop with a full ounce next time		
Desired malt flavors: Full malt flavor		Perceived malt flavor: Nice body, a little thin in the middle, but a distinct warming finish		
Desired body: Medium		Resultant body: Pretty good, just a bit watery. Might have to do with the sparging technique		
Off/Odd flavors: Just a hint of cider at the edges. Not perfect, but it won't slow me down!				
Overall impression: Pretty good IPA				
Notes/Impressions/Future goals				
Changes I'll make next time around: 1. Sparge a little more thoroughly 2. Drop in hops loose and remove through filtered siphoning 3. Get or make an immersion wort chiller! 4. Buy a racking cane and bottle filler 5. Primary-ferment in a 6-gallon (27-liter) glass carboy with blow-off tube				

Here is where you match goals with reality. Be honest or you won't know how you can improve, but don't be too hard on yourself if things don't turn out perfect. Remember, you made it, so appreciate what went right, and try to build on that.

WEB-BASED RESOURCES

There's no doubt that using the Web for some of these things can be a great boon—it is an easy way to record recipes and processes. But trust me—there is no substitute for making notes in black and white on a piece of paper. Any little changes you make on-the-fly will be lost forever unless you note them down. So as well as printing out a record of what your intentions were, make notes about what went right, what went wrong, and what you tweaked and why. These are the things that will help you become a better homebrewer.

CHAPTER 7

EXPLORE AND APPRECIATE

You've done it. Starting with simple equipment, a bit of direction, and some basic ingredients, you've made a few batches of homebrew. Some were probably better than others, but overall, you're feeling good. You've got a rhythm going. That's great! Crack open a homebrew and give yourself a toast. It's time to step things up a bit.

The following are some intermediate recipes culled from homebrew supply stores across the country. These recipes are a little more complex than the one we started with in Chapter 1. Some are partial mash, while others require the preparation of a yeast starter—and I've even thrown in a few lagers. Where possible, I've included original gravity, final gravity, and bitterness. Keep in mind that these numbers were arrived at empirically by the designers of the recipes. When you do your own calculations, you may arrive at numbers that are slightly higher. This is because calculations assume 100 percent efficiency. By comparing your calculations to the numbers in the recipes, and then to your own, you'll get an idea of the efficiency of your own system.

I have also included, in quotes, any informative notes that were given to me by the recipe designers. Any observations or information not in quotes are my additions.

EXTRACT RECIPES

BLONDE ALE

MAIDEN'S DREAM

"Maiden's dream is extra light in color and taste with a bold hop flavor. The maiden is a summer hit with all!"

ALFRED'S BREWING SUPPLY

INGREDIENTS

8 oz (225 g) pale malted grain
8 oz (225 g) pale crystal malted grain
1 tsp gypsum
$\frac{1}{2}$ oz (12 g) Chinook fresh hops (13% AA)
3 lb (1.35 kg) Dutch dry malt extract extra light
$\frac{1}{2}$ oz (12 g) Hallertau fresh hops (4.5% AA)
$\frac{1}{2}$ oz (12 g) Saaz fresh hops (3.75% AA)
American Ale Yeast
5 oz (150 g) corn sugar (priming)

OG: 1.045 FG: 1.006 ABV: 5%
IBUs: 21.5 SRM: 2.0

METHOD

Crack grain, place grain and gypsum in 1$\frac{1}{2}$ gallons (6 liters) cold water. Heat to a boil, remove grain, and discard. Add Chinook hops, boil for 40 minutes. Add all malt extract, boil for 10 minutes. Add Hallertau and Saaz hops and boil for 2 minutes. Sparge into fermenter and add cold water to 5 gallons (23 liters). When wort is below 75°F (24°C), rack to secondary fermenter for 14 days. Rack to bottling bucket, add priming sugar, and bottle.

▶ Not strictly for maidens, this homebrew is made with a mixture of pale malts.

WHEAT BEER

WARM WEATHER WHEAT (HEFEWEIZEN)

"Ah, warm weather and our thoughts turn to beaches, bare legs, and Hefeweizen! The dry extract gives a lighter color and crisper finish than the liquid. The Cascade hops are untraditional, but give the beer a nice thirst-quenching zing."

PETER A'HEARN, HOMEBREW MART

INGREDIENTS

6 lb (2.7 kg) dry wheat extract
1 oz (25 g) cascade hops (5.4% AA)
1 oz (25 g) cascade hops
Hefeweizen yeast
5 oz (150 g) corn sugar (priming)

METHOD

Add dry wheat extract to 2–3 gallons (9–14 liters) water. Bring to boil, stirring in the extract. Once hot break has subsided, add 1 oz (25 g) Cascade hops. Boil 55 minutes—add 1 oz (25 g) Cascade hops. Boil 5 minutes—shut off heat. Chill wort to 70–75°F (21–24°C). Transfer wort to primary fermenter. Top off to 5 gallons (23 liters) with cold sanitized water. Aerate well—pitch yeast. Primary-ferment for about 7 days.

Transfer to secondary fermenter, and ferment for 7 days. Bottle, using 5 oz (150 g) corn sugar. Age in bottle 7–10 days.

◀ These wheat beers require unmalted wheat or dry wheat extract to achieve their characteristic flavor.

WHEAT BEER

BELGIAN WIT ALE

*"This is the ultimate beer to make for special occasions!
This beer should be cloudy and even have a white opalescence."*

CHRIS RUSSELL, NEW YORK HOMEBREW, INC.

INGREDIENTS

8 oz (225 g) unmalted wheat

8 oz (225 g) flaked oats

4 lb (1.8 kg) liquid wheat extract

2 lb (900 g) Pilsner malt

1 lb (450 g) wheat malt

¾ oz (20 g) Crystal or Saaz hops (3% AA)

¼ oz (6 g) Crystal or Saaz hops

1 lb (450 g) light raw honey

¼ oz (6 g) coriander seed (fine crush)

⅓ oz (8 g) Curaçao (bitter) orange peel
  (chopped)

½ tsp dried ginger or 1½ tsp fresh ginger

½ tsp crushed cardamom

Belgian Wit Yeast—1 quart (1 liter) prepared
  yeast starter

5 gallons (23 liters) partial mash/extract
OG: 1.045 ABV: 4.5% IBUs: 10

METHOD

Crack grains—tie up in muslin bags. Steep grains between 150–55°F (66–8°C) for 60–75 minutes. Raise mash to 168°F (76°C)—shut off heat. Remove grains—add extract.

Bring to boil—add ¾ oz (20 g) of Crystal or Saaz hops. Boil 40 minutes—add ¼ oz (10 g) of Crystal or Saaz hops. Boil 10 minutes—add raw light honey.

Boil 5 minutes—add the coriander, orange peel, ginger, and cardamom. Boil 5 more minutes—total boiling time: 60 minutes. Shut off heat—steep for 10 minutes. Chill to 65°F (18°C) ASAP. Transfer wort to primary fermenter. Aerate well—pitch yeast.

Ferment at 60–65°F (16–18°C). No secondary fermenter used. Either bottle or keg and enjoy!

*"This is a good American-style pale ale that can be
'Hawaiianized' by adding tropical fruits before or at bottling."*

MARCI, MAUI HOMBREW SUPPLY

INGREDIENTS

1 lb (450 g) crystal malt (20L)

7 lb (3.15 kg) pale malt extract

1 oz (25 g) Northern
   Brewer hops (9% AA)

1 tsp Irish moss

½ oz (12 g) Cascade hops
   (5% AA)

American Ale Yeast

5 oz (150 g) corn sugar
   (priming)

OG: 1.050 IBUs: 30

METHOD

Place crushed grains in pot and cover with water. Heat to 150°F (66°C), and hold at that temperature for 30 minutes. Turn off heat and let stand for 15 minutes. Pour the grain into a strainer above your brew kettle. Sparge until run-off becomes clear. Discard the grain. Add the malt extract and more water, if needed, until your pot is ¾ full. Stir, occasionally. Add Northern Brewer hops and boil for 60 minutes. Continue stirring to keep syrup from sticking to the bottom of your pot. With 15 minutes left, add the Irish moss. With 5 minutes left, add Cascade hops. Boil for the final 5 minutes and remove kettle from stove. Place lid over kettle and cool wort as quickly as possible. Pour wort through a sanitized strainer into your sanitized primary fermenter. Add water (previously boiled and cooled) to equal 5 gallons (23 liters). Cover immediately. Prepare a yeast slurry. When wort is below 80°F (27°C), stir in slurry. Make sure the lid (or rubber stopper) and airlock are airtight. Ferment at approximately 70°F (21°C) until fermentation is complete (usually 5–7 days). Rack into a secondary for 10–14 days. Transfer to a bottling bucket and bottle using 5 oz (150 g) corn sugar. Aloha, and enjoy!

ENGLISH IPA

HOPPY GURKHA'S IPA

"This is a more traditional IPA than many you have tried. It has the high hop levels of an American IPA, but uses English hops, sugar, water with a high salt content, and an English ale yeast to produce a more traditional beer."

PETER A'HEARN, HOMEBREW MART

INGREDIENTS

8 oz (225 g) crystal malt (40L)
8 oz (225 g) carapils
2 tsp gypsum
8 lb (3.6 kg) pale malt extract
1 lb (450 g) golden brown sugar
1½ oz (40 g) Northdown hops (8% AA)
1 oz (25 g) Fuggles hops (4.2% AA)
English ale yeast
1 oz (25 g) first gold hops
5 oz (150 g) corn sugar (priming)

METHOD

Add grains and gypsum to ½ gallon (2 liters) of water. Raise temperature to about 155°F (68°C), and hold for 45 minutes. Sparge into brewpot. Add extract and brown sugar plus water to bring brewpot about three-quarters full. Bring to boil. When hot break subsides, add Northdown hops. With 15 munutes left, add Fuggles. After 60 minutes have expired, remove pot from heat and cool. Pitch yeast. Ferment for 6–8 days, or until bubbling has all but ceased. Rack into secondary and add first gold hops. Store for at least 5 more days, and bottle using 5 oz (150 g) corn sugar. Store an additional 10–14 days and enjoy!

◀ A single freshly picked hop.

CLASSIC STYLE

SCOTTISH ALE

"Scottish ales are known for warm inviting malt flavors and body, even in low alcohol beers like this one."

JIM MCHALE, BEER UNLIMITED

INGREDIENTS

Wyeast 1728 Scottish ale yeast

8 oz (225 g) Crystal 40 malt

2 oz (50 g) black barley

2 oz (50 g) roasted barley

3 lb (1.35kg) liquid malt extract

3 lb (1.35 kg) Pale malt extract

1 oz (25 g) East Kent Goldings hops (4.5% AA)

1 tsp Irish moss (optional)

5 oz (150 g) corn sugar (priming)

OG: 1.048 FG: 1.020 ABV: 4.13%

METHOD

For best results, make a yeast starter 24 hours before brew day. Steep grains until water begins to boil. Return to boil. Turn off heat and stir in extracts. Return to boil. When boiling starts, add 1 oz (25 g) East Kent Goldings. Boil for 60 minutes. Add Irish moss for last 30 minutes.

Pitch yeast when wort cools. Primary-ferment for 7–10 days or until finished. Bottle with priming sugar and condition 2–4 weeks.

IRISH RED ALE

EL NIÑO RED

"The Irish answer to a Scottish Ale, plenty of familiar, round malt character, but dry, crisp, and refreshing."

LYNNE O'CONNER, ST. PATRICK'S OF TEXAS BREWING SUPPLY

INGREDIENTS

2 oz (50 g) chocolate malt
1 lb (450 g) Crystal 50L malt
1 lb (450 g) Pilsner malt
1 lb (450 g) Munich malt
6 lb (2.7 kg) pale malt syrup extract
1½ oz (40 g) Challenger hops
  (7.5% AA)
1 oz (25 g) Golding hops (4.5% AA)
1 oz (25 g) Golding hops
Irish ale yeast
5 oz (150 g) corn sugar (priming)

METHOD

Add grains to ³⁄₄ gallon (3.4 liters) of water and raise temperature to anywhere between 150–58°F (66–70°C). Remove from heat, cover, and let stand for 40 minutes.

Dump contents of pot into a colander or large strainer and catch the running liquid in a pot. Sparge with ¹⁄₂ gallon (2 liters) of 170°F (77°C) water and catch this run-off as well. Discard grains. Stir in extract, until it is completely dissolved. Add more water if necessary. Bring to a boil. When hot break subsides, add Challenger hops. With 10 minutes left, add 1 oz (25 g) Golding hops. With 1 minute left, add 1 oz (25 g) Golding hops. Remove from heat and quickly cool. Pitch with prepared yeast packet and primary-ferment for 6–8 days. Rack to secondary and store for an additional 7–10 days. Bottle using 5 oz (150 g) priming sugar. Save for a tempest-tossed day, and enjoy!

● CLASSIC STYLE ●

PORTER

"This particular recipe took first place in the 1997 war of the worts competition. If your local supplier doesn't carry the specific ingredients, ask him for substitutes."

JIM MCHALE, BEER UNLIMITED

INGREDIENTS

Irish ale yeast
8 oz (225 g) Crystal 40L Malt
8 oz (225 g) chocolate malt
4 oz (115 g) black malt
2 lbs Amber Dry Malt Extract
3 lbs Pale Liquid Malt Extract
1 oz (25 g) Nugget hops (13% AA)
1 tsp Irish moss
2 oz (50 g) Willamette hops (5% AA)
5 oz (150 g) corn sugar (priming)

OG: 1.050 FG: 1.016 ABV: 4.39%

METHOD

Prepare a yeast starter 24 hours before brew day. Steep grains until water begins to boil. Remove grains. Turn off heat and stir in extracts. Return to boil. When boiling starts, add 1 oz (25g) nugget hops. Boil for 60 minutes. Add Irish moss (optional) for last 30 minutes. Add 1 oz (25 g) Willamette hops for last 2 minutes. Cool wort quickly, and pitch yeast starter.

Primary-ferment for 7–10 days. Dry-hop with the final 1 oz (25 g) of Willamette. (Add hops to primary fermenter two days before racking.) Rack to secondary for an additional 7 days. Bottle with 5 oz (150 g) priming sugar. Store bottles for a week or two, and enjoy!

"This beer is dark and dry with notes of chocolate and espresso."

JIM MCHALE, BEER UNLIMITED

INGREDIENTS

Irish Ale Yeast

1 lb (450 g) roasted barley

1 lb (450 g) black barley (not
    black patent)

6 lbs dark liquid malt extract

3 lbs Pale Liquid Malt Extract

2 oz (50 g) East Kent Goldings hops
    (4.5% AA)

1 tsp Irish moss

1 oz (25 g) Challenger hops (7.5% AA)

5 oz (150 g) corn sugar (priming)

OG: 1.052 FG: 1.014 ABV: 4.90%

METHOD

Remove pitchable yeast from the refrigerator.
No other preparation is necessary with
pitchable yeast. Steep grains until water
begins to boil. Remove grains. Turn off heat
and stir in extracts. Return to boil. When boil
starts, add 2 oz (50 g) East Kent Golding hops.
Boil for 60 minutes. Add Irish moss for last 30
minutes. Add ½ oz (12 g) Challenger hops for
last 15 minutes. Add ½ oz (12 g) Challenger
hops for last 2 minutes. Cool wort quickly and
pitch yeast. Primary-ferment for 5–8 days or
until complete. Rack to secondary for an
additional 5 days. Prime with 5 oz (150 g)
corn sugar and bottle. Enjoy!

LIGHT LAGER

BOHEMIAN PILSNER

"Modeled after Pilsner Urquell, this beer combines a light, but present, malt character with the floral spiciness of Saaz hops."

JIM MCHALE, BEER UNLIMITED

INGREDIENTS

Czech Pils lager yeast

3 lb pale liquid malt extract

3 lb (1.35 kg) extra-light dry malt extract

1 oz (25 g) Saaz hops (bittering)

1 tsp Irish moss

2 oz (50 g) Saaz hops (flavor and aroma)

1 tbsp gelatin

5 oz (150 g) corn sugar (priming)

OG: 1.048 FG: 1.012 ABV: 4.64%

METHOD

Pop yeast packet 48 days before brew day. Prepare yeast starter 24 hours before brew day. Bring water to a boil. Turn off the heat and stir in extracts. Return to a boil. When boiling starts add bittering Saaz. Boil for 60 minutes total. Add Irish moss for the last 30 minutes. Add ½ oz (12 g) Saaz hops for the last 15 minutes. Add ½ oz (12 g) Saaz hops for the last 5 minutes. Cool wort quickly and pitch yeast starter. Primary-ferment at 50°F (10°C) for 10–14 days. Rack to secondary. Dry-hop with 1 oz (25 g) Saaz hops.

Lager for 4–6 weeks at 40–45°F (4–7°C). Add gelatin 2 days before bottling. Bottle with priming sugar and store cool for as long as you can stand (varies with individual). Drink and enjoy!

DARK LAGER

DOPPLEBOCK

"This recipe is fairly simple to put together, but since it is a true partial mash and may even be your first attempt at a lager, I have written out a short set of special instructions to keep in mind. Happy brewing!"

CHRIS RUSSELL, NEW YORK HOMEBREW, INC.

INGREDIENTS

12 oz (350 g) Belgian special "B" malt
4 oz (115 g) Carafa malt
6¹⁄₂ lb (3 kg) Amber Extract
1¹⁄₂ lb (700 g) Dark Munich malt
³⁄₄ oz (20 g) Perle hops (7.5% AA)
¹⁄₂ oz (12 g) German Hallertau hops
  (4.5% AA)
Lager yeast—1 quart (1 liter) prepared
  yeast starter

OG: 1.068 ABV: 6% IBUs: 24

METHOD

Crack grains, tie up in muslin bags. Steep grains at 152–156°F (67–69°C) for 45 minutes. Raise mash to 168°F (76°C). Turn off heat. Remove grains and stir in extracts. Return to a boil. When boiling, add Perle hops. Boil 50 minutes, add German Hallertau hops. Boil 10 more minutes—total boiling time is 60 minutes. Turn off heat and cool wort to 65°F (18°C), ASAP. Aerate wort well and pitch yeast starter. Primary-ferment at 55–60°F (13–16°C). Rack to secondary fermenter. Maintain secondary at approximately 40°F (4°C) for 1 month. Either bottle or keg and enjoy!

STEAM BEER

CALIFORNIA COMMON

"Everyone who brews this style tries to copy Anchor Steam, the standard for the style. This is a different kind of California Common than Anchor—especially with the hop schedule. Let's call it California Un-common."

LISA HADDOCK, BEER UNLIMITED

INGREDIENTS

California lager yeast
8 oz (225 g) Caramunich II
6 lbs of pale liquid malt extract
1 oz (25 g) Chinook hops (13% AA)
1 tsp Irish moss
½ oz (12 g) Hallertau Hersbrucker hops
  (3.5% AA)
1 oz (25 g) Northern Brewer hops (9% AA)
5 oz (150 g) corn sugar (priming)

OG: 1.045 FG: 1.008 ABV: 4.77%

METHOD

Pop yeast packet 48 days before brew day. Prepare yeast starter 24 hours before brew day. Steep grains until water begins to boil. Remove grains. Remove from heat and stir in Northwestern extract. Return to a boil. When boil recommences add ½ oz (12 g) Chinook hops. This will be boiled for the full 60 minutes. Add ½ oz (12 g) Chinook hops for last 40 minutes. Add Irish moss for last 30 minutes. Add Hallertau hops for last 20 minutes. Add Northern Brewer at end of boil. Cool wort quickly and pitch yeast. Primary-ferment for 7–10 days at 65–70°F (18–21°C). Rack to secondary and ferment for 14 days at 45–50°F (7–10°C). Bottle, using corn sugar. Age in bottle for 7–10 days.

FRUIT BEER

RASPBERRY AMBER

"The fruit purée is aseptic so you don't have to worry about contamination. For a more intriguing brew, try using White Labs Trappist ale yeast."

PETER A'HEARN, HOMEBREW MART

INGREDIENTS

1 lb (450 g) Crystal 60L malt
7 lb (3.15 kg) pale malt extract
1 oz (25 g) Progress hops (5.7% AA)
White Labs British ale yeast
1 can Oregon brand raspberry purée
5 oz (150 g) corn sugar (priming)

METHOD

Add grains to water and heat to a boil. Remove grains. Remove from heat and stir in extract. Return to a boil. When wort is boiling, add 1 oz (25 g) progress hops (60 minutes in boil). Add remaining 1 oz (25 g) progress hops during last 5 minutes of boil.

Cool wort quickly and pitch yeast. Primary-ferment for 7–10 days. Rack to secondary and add purée. Leave in secondary for 7 days. Bottle with 5oz (150 g) corn sugar.

◀ Freshly picked raspberries.

ALL-GRAIN RECIPES

SWEET STOUT

GRANNY'S SECRET

"My grandmother was taken to church, aged seven, and encouraged to swear an oath never to let alcohol pass her lips. Ninety years have passed and she has kept her promise. But for the oath, this is the beer I think she would have liked."

ANTONY HAYES, WWW.ANTHAYES.COM

INGREDIENTS

4 lb 13 oz (2.2 kg) Pale malt
15 oz (425 g) Wheat malt
9 oz (250 g) Black malt
9 oz (250 g) Lactose
1$^{1}/_{10}$ oz (32 g) Fuggle (4.5% AA) for
   60 minutes
Windsor ale yeast

5$^{1}/_{4}$ gallons (23.9 liters)
OG: 1.037 FG: 1.014 IBUs: 20

METHOD

If using a liquor correction, reduce your water's total alkalinity to 100–150 ppm (as $CaCO_3$). Then adjust calcium content to 100–120 p.p.m. using calcium chloride. Mash in at 154°F (68°C) and hold to starch conversion. Mash-out at 169°F (76°C). Boil for 90 minutes. Ferment at around 64°F (18°C).

◀ Pale malt provides the base for this delicious homebrew recipe.

• CLASSIC STYLE •

BEST BITTER

"This is an adapted version of the 'Black Spot Bitter' recipe that won first place in the 2010 Brew Whart / Beermerchants.com homebrew competition."

MARK CHARLWOOD, BEERBIRRABIER.BLOGSPOT.COM

INGREDIENTS

8 lb 11 oz (3.9 kg) Pale Malt
6¹/₂ oz (191 g) Crystal 120
3³/₄ oz (106 g) Flaked Barley
1 oz (25 g) Roast Barley
2 oz (50 g) East Kent Goldings (5.1% AA) at 60 minutes
¹/₂ oz (12 g) East Kent Goldings (5.1% AA) at 15 minutes
Add Irish Moss at 15 minutes
1 oz (25 g) Fuggle (4.9%AA) at 1 minute
Safale S-04 (dry yeast)

5¹/₄ gallons (23.8 liters)
OG: 1.050 FG: 1.009 ABV: 5.6% IBUs: 36

METHOD

Mash at 153°F (67°C) for 60 minutes, sparge and collect 5¹/₄ gallons. Boil for 60 minutes, making additions to schedule. Cool to 86°F (30°C), aerate, and pitch at 73°F (23°C). Ferment 7–10 days at 66°F (19°C), rack to secondary for 7 days.

▶ Flaked barley.

DARK LAGER

HIBERNATOR DOPPELBOCK

"A nice big warm lager to lay down over the winter with."

LEE BIRKETT, WWW.UKBREWER.COM

INGREDIENTS

12 lb 4 oz (5.57 kg) Munich Type II
4 lb 11 oz (2.14 kg) Pilsner malt
1 lb 11 oz (772 g) Caramunich Type III
3 oz (86 g) Pale Chocolate Malt
$1/2$ oz (12g) Perle (8.2% AA) added at
   60 minutes
$^{1}/_{2}$ oz (12 g) Perle (8.2% AA) added at
   30 minutes
1 Whirlfloc Tablet / Irish moss, added at
   20 minutes
1 tsp Wyeast Nutrient, added at 15 minutes
$^{1}/_{4}$ oz (7 g) Tettnanger (4.5% AA) added at
   15 minutes
Bavarian Lager or Oktoberfest Lager Yeast

OG: 1.080 FG: 1.020 ABV: 7.9% IBUs: 22

▶ Wyeast Nutrient gives this recipe the
necessary chemical reactions to ensure
a professional full flavor.

METHOD

Prepare yeast starter (at least 2 liters) prior
to brewday. Mash at 153°F (67°C) for 60
minutes. Mash out at 167°F (75°C), sparge
and collect 6 gallons (27.3 liters). Boil for 90
minutes, making additions to schedule.
Chill to 50°F (10°C), aerate aggressively and
pitch yeast. Primary ferment for 3 weeks,
transfer to secondary and lager for 6–8 weeks.

NOTE: This recipe recommends a yeast
starter prepared a couple of days in advance.

AMERICAN IPA

BABY-FACED ASSASSIN

"This uses a fairly radical approach to hopping to produce an American IPA-style beer of exceptional intensity, showcasing the beauty of the Citra hop. Because of the large volume of hops, expect to lose quite a few pints of wort through absorption. The predicted IBUs are quite high, but Citra has a fairly soft bittering profile, despite their high % alpha acid."

TOM FOZARD, WWW.TWITTER.COM/CHEEESEBOIGER

INGREDIENTS

14 lb 5 oz (6.5 kg) Maris Otter pale malt

2 oz (50 g) Crystal malt 60l

5 oz (150 g) Citra (13.8% AA) added at 10 minutes

5½ oz (175 g) Citra (13.8% AA) added at 1 minute

2½ oz (75g) Citra (13.8% AA) added at flame out, and steep for 30 minutes

Safale S-04 (dry ale yeast)

6½ gallons (30 liters)
OG: 1.066 FG: 1.018 ABV: 6.4% IBUs: 70

METHOD

Mash at 153°F (67°C) for 60 minutes, then sparge and collect 6½ gallons (30 liters). Boil for 60 minutes, making additions to schedule.

Cool to 86°F (30°C), aerate and pitch at around 77°F (25°C). Ferment for 7 days at 66°F (19°C).

IRISH RED ALE

REINVENTED RED

"As an Irish brewer and beer geek I find Irish Red ale to be infuriating. It is not a traditional Irish style of beer, but is rather what has become of Irish ale after decades of brewery consolidations and dumbing down. As a 'style' it is characterized by not having much in the way of hop, malt, or yeast character. The following beer is what I think Irish Red Ale should be. It has both malt and hop character, so it is not to style. As a result, I enjoy drinking it."

SÉAN BILLINGS, WWW.BEOIR.ORG

INGRDIENTS

6 lb 6 oz (2.9 kg) pale malt

1½ lb (400 g) Crystal 55L (145 EBC)

1½ oz (40 g) roasted barley

¾ oz (20 g) Challenger (8% AA) at 60 minutes

⅔ oz (16 g) First Gold (5.4% AA) at 20 minutes

⅔ oz (16 g) First Gold (5.4% AA) at 5 minutes

⅓ oz (8 g) First Gold (5.4% AA) at flame out

Irish Ale Yeast

6 gallons (27.3 liters)

OG: 1.044 FG: 1.012 ABV: 4.5% IBUs: 34

METHOD

Mash at 51°F (66°C) for 60 minutes, then sparge and collect 6 gallons (27.3 liters). Boil for 60 minutes, making additions to schedule.

Cool to 86°F (30°C), aerate and pitch around 77 F (25°C). Ferment for 7 days at 66°F (19°C).

• INDIA PALE ALE •

AMBER SAMSARA

"I'm fascinated by the dialogue between British and American brewing cultures, and so this is a hybrid between a pale golden English ale (Summer Lightning is a classic) and an American IPA (a pale one like Dogfish Head 60 Minute). The amber malt gives this beer a subtle background note."

ZAK AVERY, THEBEERBOY.BLOGSPOT.COM

INGREDIENTS

11 lb (5 kg) Maris Otter pale malt
4½ oz (125 g) Amber Malt (Fawcett's)
¾ oz (20 g) Challenger (8% AA) at 60 minutes
⅔ oz (16 g) First Gold (5.4% AA) at
    20 minutes
⅔ oz (16 g) First Gold (5.4% AA) at 5 minutes
⅓ oz (8 g) First Gold (5.4% AA) at flame out
Irish Ale Yeast

5½ gallons (25 liters)
OG: 1.066 FG: 1.018 ABV: 6.5% IBUs: 50

METHOD

Mash at 153°F (67°C) for 60 minutes, sparge and collect 5½ gallons (25 liters). Boil for 60 minutes, making additions to schedule.

Cool, aerate and pitch around 77°F (25°C). Ferment 7–10 days.

▶ A single golden hop.

"While not as strong or as heavily bitter as some American IPAs, this all-grain recipe uses a series of late hop additions to build up as much classic C-hop flavor and aroma as possible, while delivering a reasonable dose of bitterness at about 55 IBUs. Note that as this uses a lot of pellet hops, you may want to consider using a hop sock to minimize loss of wort."

BARRY MASTERSON, THEBITTENBULLET.BLOGSPOT.COM

INGREDIENTS

9½ lb (4.3 kg) pale malt
1 lb (450 g) malted wheat
1 lb (450 g) Munich malt
¾ lb (340 g) crystal malt
½ oz (12 g) Chinook hop pellets (11.2% AA) at 60 minutes
½ oz (12 g) Chinook hop pellets (11.2% AA) at 30 minutes
½ oz (12 g) Centennial hop pellets (9.7% AA) at 20 minutes
½ oz (12 g) Centennial hop pellets (9.7% AA) at 15 minutes
1 tsp Irish Moss at 15 minutes
½ oz (12 g) Cascade hop pellets (6.6% AA) at 10 minutes
½ oz (12 g) Cascade hop pellets (6.6% AA) at 5 minutes
½ oz (12 g) Cascade hop pellets (6.6% AA) at flame out
Fermentis S-05 American Ale Yeast

OG: 1.058 FG: 1.015 ABV: 5.7% IBUs: 55

METHOD

Mash at 155°F (68°C) for 60 minutes, batch sparge at 176°F (80°C) and collect 5½ gallons (25 liters). Boil for 60 minutes, making additions to schedule

Cool to 75°F (24°C), aerate and pitch hydrated yeast. Ferment 7–14 days at 65–68°F (18–20°C).

"A dark, easy drinking beer, with subtle fruity hops over a smooth malty base."

ADRIAN CHAPMAN, PDTNC.WORDPRESS.COM

INGREDIENTS

6 lb 4 oz (2.84 kg) Pale Malt
14¼ oz (405 g) Crystal 120
14¼ oz (405 g) Munich malt
8½ oz (240 g) flaked oats
2⅘ oz (81 g) chocolate malt
2⅘ oz (81 g) chocolate wheat malt
¾ oz (20 g) Golding (4.2% AA) at 60 minutes
¾ oz (20 g) Fuggle (3.9% AA) at 60 minutes
Irish Moss at 15 minutes
½ oz (12 g) Golding (4.2% AA) at 60 minutes
½ oz (12 g) Fuggle (3.9% AA) at 60 minutes
Fermentis Safale S-04 (dry)

6 gallons (27.3 liters)
OG: 1.058 FG: 1.015 ABV: 5.7% IBUs: 55

METHOD

Mash at 154–156°F (68–69°C) in 2½ gallons (9.5 liters) for 60 minutes, sparge and collect 6 gallons (27.3 liters). Boil for 60 minutes, making additions to schedule.

Cool to 77°F (25°C), aerate, and pitch Ferment 7–10 days at 66°F (19°C).

▶ You can reuse your bottles again and again. Simply wash them as soon as you've poured to avoid having to clean hardened sediment out a few hours later.

ASSESSING YOUR BREW

Listen for the healthy sound of escaping CO_2 as you open the bottle. Watch as the bubbles rush to the surface. Note the clarity and color of the brew. Smell the array of aromas, and learn to discern the many flavors of beer. Most of all, enjoy your beer!

Homebrewers Associations host and sponsor many competitions every year. Entering your beer into a competition will give you an objective assessment of the quality of your homebrew, and the certified judges will offer ways to improve your beer.

You can use the same criteria at home to evaluate your beer. A simple test, as suggested by homebrew experts such as Charlie Papazian, Dave Miller, Gregg Smith, and Fred Edhardt, utilizes a 20-point system, broken down as follows:

1. Bouquet and aroma: 0–4 points
   Hop bouquet
   Aroma from malt, other fermentables
2. Appearance: 0–3 points
   Clarity
   Color
   Head retention
3. Taste: 10 points
   Balance between malt and hops
   Mouth-feel (light–heavy)
   Aftertaste
4. Overall impression: 1–3 points
   Does the beer represent its style?
   Is it drinkable?
   Are there any off flavors?

▲ Learning to assess your homebrew is an important step toward achieving consistency.

The easiest way to learn recipe formulation is to find a homebrew recipe and play with it. The two major factors involved in how your beer will turn out are technique and ingredients. Hone the first by brewing a single recipe until you achieve consistent results. Then, substitute one ingredient at a time, keeping detailed notes on how the beer looks, tastes, etc. For example, if you are brewing Hoppy Gurkha's IPA, try a darker- or lighter-colored crystal malt. Substitute dry extract for syrup (making the appropriate quantity adjustment). Change the yeast strain to a liquid, or change the variety of hops. Make only one change per batch and record differences in outcome. Your technique will also alter your homebrew. By replacing a percentage of extract with a compatible grain, your brew will turn out different. Partial-mash brewers have the advantage of freshness and control, though considerations such as extract yield must be taken into account. Preparing a yeast starter may result in a more highly attenuated brew. The addition of a wort chiller to your system can aid in clarity and flavor. Altering hopping schedules will affect the bitterness and flavor, as will the form of hops that you are using. Specific gravity, color, and bitterness are the three factors to consider when devising your own recipe or experimenting with published recipes. If you are brewing a specific style, you'll want to stay within the parameters of that style.

GRAVITY

The specific gravity of a wort is the measurement of all the fermentable and unfermentable sugars swimming around in your fermenter at a given time. Original gravity is the amount before fermentation, and final gravity is the amount remaining after the yeast has metabolized much of the matter. All malts and adjuncts add varying amounts of gravity, or density, to your wort. They don't, however, all proffer the same amount of sugars, nor do they all contribute identical flavor. The variety of malt (six-row or two-row), the degree of modification, and the amount of time spent in the kiln all determine the flavor, color, and gravity. Likewise, adjuncts and other fermentables each have their own characteristics.

There are, however, a few basic malts that generally make up the bulk of fermentable compounds in all styles of beer. A loose but somewhat fitting analogy is to compare these grains to a pizza crust. There are only a few types of crust. Yet everyone has a favorite type of pizza. Some like pepperoni, some mushroom, and some sausage. There is a huge variety of pizzas available, but each must have some basic crust underneath to support the sauces, cheese, and toppings. If adjuncts and specialty grains help distinguish different styles of beer, then basic brewer's malt is the crust that makes it all possible. Lager and Pilsner malts are the basis for lagers: the former for pale and dark lagers, as well as some ales, and the latter for Pilsners and other light lagers. Pale-ale malt constitutes a large portion of the grain bill in most British ales, from pale to porter. The sweeter and somewhat deeper-colored Vienna malt is often used as the basis for Oktoberfest and Marzen lagers. The amber, aromatic Munich malt is used in some German lagers, and as a flavoring malt in many other beers, and other wheat beers.

When you purchase an extract, you are often getting a combination of one of the above malts with some percentage of specialty malt. While a light malt extract may be mainly composed of mashed pale malt, dark malt extract may be a blend of pale malt with darker specialty malts, such as chocolate or roasted malt. Hence the all-extract brewer can produce a dark stout without adding specialty grains. However, note that even the darkest extract is prepared with mostly two-row pale-ale malt, and then colored with dark crystal, black patent, or chocolate malt. None of these constitute most of the extract,

because none contains the starch converting enzymes for a proper mash.

When I partial-mash, I like to use lighter extracts and add malts to attain body, color, and flavor. For example, I may substitute a portion of extract for pale-ale malt when making a stout. Then I can add a pound or so of dark specialty malt to achieve proper color. Consult the Malt Profiles table (page 198) for a description of various malts.

▲ A home bar allows you to serve your homebrew from the tap.

SWAPPING MALTS

You can easily use dry malt extract in a recipe calling for extract syrup, and vice versa. Since syrup contains up to 20 percent water, it supplies less gravity per pound than DME. If a recipe calls for DME, multiply the amount by 1.2 for how much syrup to use. Or, if a recipe calls for extract syrup, multiply the amount by 0.8 for how much DME to add.

You can also replace a portion of extract with grain. However, simply replacing a pound of extract with 1 lb (450 g) of pale-ale malt will result in a lower OG. Whenever you mash and sparge, you inevitably leave some fermentables behind. If you want to substitute malt for a portion of your extract, use the following formulas.

TO CONVERT EXTRACT TO GRAIN:

1 lb (450 g) malt extract syrup x 1.23 = 1 lb (450 g) pale malt
1 lb (450 g) dry malt extract x 1.45 = 1 lb (450 g) pale malt
1 lb (450 g) wheat malt extract x 1.07 = 1 lb (450 g) wheat malt

To find out how much extract to use in place of malt, use the following formula:

1 lb (450 g) pale malt x 0.8125 = 1 lb (450 g) malt extract syrup
1 lb (450 g) pale malt x 0.6875 = 1 lb (450 g) dry malt extract
1 lb (450 g) wheat malt x 0.937 = 1 lb (450 g) wheat malt extract

Say you have a recipe that calls for 6.6 lb (3 kg) liquid malt extract, and you want to substitute 1 lb (450 g) of pale malt. How much extract would you need to add to achieve the same original gravity? First, convert the 1 lb (450 g) of malt to extract using the formula:

1 lb (450 g) pale malt x 0.8125 = 1 lb (450 g) malt extract syrup

So, 1 lb (450 g) of pale malt x 0.8125 = 0.8125 lb malt extract syrup. Next, subtract the product from the total extract, to find the extract needed to get the same OG:

6/6—0.8125 = 5.36 lb malt extract syrup

For the record, it's a lot easier to weigh dry malt extract than it is to weigh extract syrup.

BITTERNESS

While the degree of bitterness may vary from style to style, all beer is balanced with hops. Bitterness is the result of isomerized alpha acids, which dissolve into solution during the boil. To calculate bitterness, measured as IBUs, use the Hop Utilization table on page 207. By looking up IBUs in the Beer Style Guidelines table in the same section, you can devise a hopping schedule that matches the parameters of your chosen style.

When devising recipes, some brewers go over the top with hops. So-called "hop heads," dizzy with a love of the bittering flower, add lupulin with a lupine appetite. However, too much of a good thing can cause a harsh bite that borders on astringency. Stay cool, beware the moon, and don't overdo it with the hops.

Higher-gravity beers tolerate heavy hop additions better than lighter brews. The reason is simple. Higher gravities mean more sugars, which means more sweetness to absorb the bitterness of the hop. A barley wine or imperial stout is highly hopped to counterbalance the huge malt additions.

▼ Hops are available pressed into pellet form for ease of use.

FLAVOR AND BOUQUET

While all hops contain essential oils, certain varieties are cultivated to supply distinctive hop aromas and flavors. Cascade, Kent Goldings, and Saaz hops come to mind. Each variety is prized for its aromatic properties, yet each has a unique flavor that testifies to the range and complexity found within the plant's lupulin glands. Kent Goldings hops distinguish British pale ales from all others. The classic, mild flavors are in stark contrast to those of the floral, citrusy Cascade hop—a popular finishing hop in American pale ales. No one can deny the signature that the Saaz hop gives to Bohemian Pilsners. The spicy aroma and flavor make it truly unique.

When choosing a finishing hop, decide what quality or qualities you want to achieve. Volatile oils are lost quickly, so purchase only the freshest hops that are sealed in nitrogen-purged bags and stored under refrigeration. Confine your additions to late in the boil, add them directly after the boil, or dry-hop in a secondary fermenter.

Most of all, experiment with different varieties of hops until you perceive how each affects the aroma and flavor of your homebrew. All of the descriptive adjectives and similes in the world fail to convey what your senses will tell you through experience.

COLOR

Color is determined by the type of malt used, the length and intensity of the boil, the rate of cooling to pitching temperatures, the strain of yeast used, and a number of other factors. In the intermediate section, I showed you a simple and popular method for predicting final color, based on the Lovibond rating assigned to each malt. This formula will give you a rough estimate of how light or dark your beer will be, based on Homebrew Color Units. This scale, however, doesn't correspond very well with the SRM color scale. Still, in the absence of expensive equipment or access to a lab, HCUs offer some approximation. Color is, perhaps, the most difficult quality to predict and quantify. Using the Malt Profiles table in the back of the book, along with the simple HCU formula, will give you a starting point. Experience will serve to sharpen your intuition. Homebrewing is a blend of science and art. When science is beyond your means, you need to hone your artistic sensibilities.

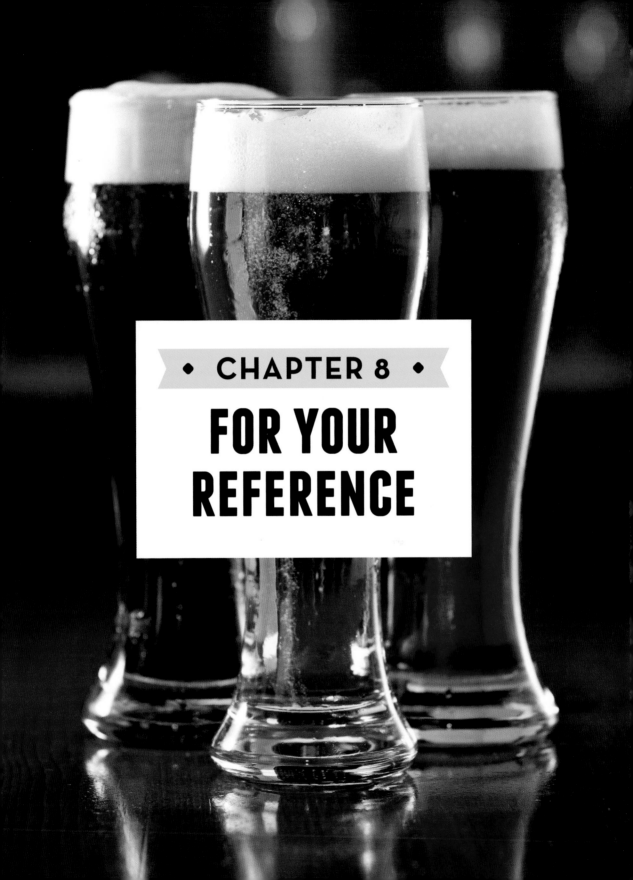

CHAPTER 8

FOR YOUR REFERENCE

I love to cook. Always have. When I was younger, my version of cooking meant following whatever recipe was in front of me to a T, and I got a lot of enjoyment out of achieving a result that was faithful to the type of dish I was attempting. As I started getting more consistent results, I began to improvise. Nothing too dramatic—an extra pinch here, a dash there. But it wasn't until I started understanding the nature of each ingredient that my cooking started taking off.

Think of this section as a way to start learning about the nature of each ingredient that goes into making beer. This is not something that needs to be mastered all at once. Let the information come naturally as you continue to enjoy your craft. Before you know it, you'll have a level of familiarity that will give you the knowledge and confidence to start riffing.

The following tables will help you understand how ingredients contribute to the final characteristics of your homebrew and are a starting point for concocting your own recipes. While these formulas also appear in earlier chapters, they are compiled here for an easy reference when filling out your Homebrew Worksheets.

DETERMINING SPECIFIC GRAVITY

Using Tables 3 and 4, you can gain a rough estimate of the original gravity that various malts, adjuncts, and sugars will give to your wort. As a general rule, you can assume that the final gravity will be approximately one-quarter that of the original gravity.

SG of fermentable x lbs added
+ SG of fermentable x lbs added
Volume of beer brewed = OG

SWAPPING MALTS

Extract to Extract:
1 lb (450 g) malt syrup extract = 0.8 lb (360 g) dry malt extract
1 lb (450 g) dry malt extract = 1.2 lb (540 g) malt extract syrup

Extract to Grain:
lbs malt extract syrup x 1.23 = lbs pale malt
lbs dry malt extract x 1.45 = lbs pale malt
lbs wheat malt extract x 1.07 = lbs wheat malt

Grain to Extract:
lbs pale malt x 0.8125 = lbs malt extract syrup
lbs pale malt x 0.6875 = lbs dry malt extract
lbs wheat malt x 0.937 = lbs wheat malt

DETERMINING APPARENT ATTENUATION PERCENTAGE

APP = [(original gravity—final gravity) / original gravity] x 100

PREDICTING BITTERNESS

Use Glenn Tinseth's Hop Utilization Table on page 207 to find alpha acid utilization rated based on wort gravity and time hops spend in the boil.

IBUs = decimal alpha acid utilization x mg/l of added alpha acids

To calculate mg/l of added alpha acids, use:

Decimal AA rating x oz hops x 7490
Volume of finished beer in gallons = mg/l of added alpha acids

TABLE 1: BEER STYLE GUIDELINES

Key:
OG = Original Gravity
FG = Final Gravity
IBUs = International Bittering Units
SRM = Standard Reference Measurement

Beer Style	OG	FG	IBUs	SRM
Ales				
Belgian strong ale	1.062–1.095	1.011–1.023	20–50	3–7 (light)
				7–20 (dark)
Flanders brown	1.040–1.055	1.006–1.015	10–25	10–20
Lambic	1.045–1.056	1.000–1.010	11–23	6–14
Belgian pale ale	1.044–1.096	1.008–1.024	25–45	4–12
Trappist	1.044–1.096	1.008–1.024	25–45	4–12
Dubbel	1.050–1.070	1.012–1.016	18–30	10–18
Trippel	1.065–1.096	1.018–1.024	18–30	4–7
Wit	1.044–1.050	1.006–1.010	18–28	2–4
Barley wine	1.085–1.120	1.024–1.032	50–100	14–30
Bitter	1.035–1.050	1.006–1.014	25–55	8–12
English IPA	1.050–1.068	1.012–1.018	40–60	6–18
English pale ale	1.044–1.056	1.008–1.016	20–40	4–11
Porter	1.045–1.060	1.008–1.016	25–40	30+
Scottish ales	1.035–1.050	1.010–1.018	10–25	10–25
Scotch ale	1.072–1.085	1.016–1.028	25–35	10–30
Stout (dry)	1.038–1.045	1.008–1.014	30–40	40+
Stout (sweet)	1.045–1.056	1.012–1.020	15–25	40+
Imperial stout	1.075–1.095	1.020–1.032	50–85	20+

Beer Style	OG	FG	IBUs	SRM
Strong ale/English old ale	1.055–1.125	1.010–1.040	25–75	15–20
Bière de Garde	1.060–1.077	1.012–1.014	25–30	8–12
Alt	1.042–1.050	1.006–1.014	28–45	11–19
Dunkenweizen	1.046–1.056	1.008–1.016	10–15	11–18
Hefeweizen	1.046–1.056	1.008–1.016	10–15	3–9
Weizen	1.046–1.056	1.008–1.016	10–15	3–9
Weizenbock	1.066–1.080	1.016–1.028	10–15	7–30
American pale ale	1.044–1.056	1.008–1.016	20–40	4–1
American IPA	1.052–1.070	1.012–1.018	40–65	8–14

Beer Style	OG	FG	IBUs	SRM
Lagers				
Vienna	1.048–1.056	1.012–1.018	22–28	8–12
Bohemian Pilsner	1.044–1.056	1.014–1.020	30–45	3–5
Bock	1.066–1.074	1.018–1.024	20–30	18–28
Doppelbock	1.074–1.082	1.020–1.030	17–27	12–30
Helles Bock	1.066–1.068	1.012–1.020	20–35	4–8
Dortmunder	1.048–1.056	1.010–1.014	20–38	3–6
Munich dunkel	1.050–1.056	1.012–1.018	18–27	14–20
Munich Helles	1.044–1.052	1.008–1.012	20–30	4–6
German Pilsner	1.048–1.050	1.006–1.012	30–40	3–4
Rauchbier	1.048–1.052	1.012–1.016	20–30	10–20
Schwarzbier	1.044–1.052	1.012–1.016	20–30	25–30
California common	1.042–1.055	1.012–1.018	35–45	8–17

TABLE 2: MALT PROFILES

Potential extract for 1 lb (450 g) malt in 1 gallon (4.5 liters) of water at 60°F (16°C), the following malts can be used to 100 percent in all grain brewing and must be mashed.

Malt & Country	SG	SRM	Description
2-row pale malt US	1.037	2–4	Well modified with a high diastatic power. Can be substituted for light malt extract in partial mashing. Often used for ales and lagers.
6-row pale malt US	1.035	1–2	High enzyme content makes it a good partner in a high-adjunct mash. Considered inferior to 2-row variety in flavor and clarity.
Lager malt (Klages) US	1.036	1–2	Can be substituted for a portion of extract in the production of lagers.
Pilsner malt Europe	1.036	1–2	Low enzyme content and large husk-to-starch ratio prohibits partial-mash additions beyond 20 percent of total grain bill. Often used in Pilsners and Bocks.
2-row pale ale malt Belgium, Britain	1.037	1–2	Relatively low in enzymes, this malt can, nonetheless, convert well using a single-infusion mash. Used in the production of all British ales.
Vienna malt Europe, US, Canada	1.036	4–5	Amber and sweet, this malt is used in Vienna, Marzen, and Oktoberfest lagers.
Mild ale malt Britain	1.036	3–6	This is pale ale malt that has been further kilned to deepen husk color. Mild malt imparts a sweet nutty flavor to dark British ales, like milds and browns.
Munich malt Europe, US, Canada	1.036	5–10	Similar to the mild ale, this malt gives beers a deep orange-reddish color and imparts a rich aroma and toasted-grain taste.
Wheat malt Europe, US	1.038	1–3	Can be used in small quantities for partial mash brewing. Used in the production of wheat beers, and in small amounts to aid in head retention. For single-infusion mashing, use wheat malt extract for the bulk of your grist.

The following specialty malts and grains contribute various characteristics to your beer, but do not need to be mashed.

Grain	SG	SRM	Description
CaraPils/Dextrine malt	1.033	1–2	Used to enhance body in lighter beers without imparting appreciable color. Slow kilning keeps this crystal malt light.
Victory malt	1.036	3–5	Used in dark ales and lagers to add a toasty flavor.
Light crystal malt	1.033	10–25	Both light and dark crystal malts add sweetness, body from dextrins, and color to a variety of ales. These specialty malts are popular in pale ales and IPAs. Check the packaging for specific Lovibond ratings.
Dark crystal malt	1.031	60–150	See above.
Biscuit malt	1.035	23–50	Used in brown ales and other dark beers. Imparts a warm, toasty, biscuitlike flavor.
Chocolate malt	1.032	325–450	Pale malt is roasted until a chocolate color is reached. Lends a roasted flavor to dark ales, like porter and stout.
Black patent malt	1.030	500–700	Also used in porters and stouts, this malt is kilned longer than chocolate malt, resulting in the charcoal-black color. Used in small amounts for coloring and lending a burnt, sometimes bitter flavor.
Roasted barley	1.035	400–500	Similar to black patent, this unmalted barley is drier in flavor and aroma. Can impart coffee-like flavors to dry stouts, and is used to deepen the color of mild and Scottish ales.

The following is a list of both dry and syrup malt extracts. Ask your local supplier for information on specific brands. Also, consult the manufacturer and other homebrewers to find which brand delivers the best and most consistent results. While some people find it easier to work with syrup (it doesn't clump in the wort), DME has a longer shelf life and is more potent. Finally, make sure your extract is marked "unhopped" before you buy it. This gives you more control over the destiny of your homebrew!

Extract	SG	SRM	Description
Light syrup	1.040	3–6	While many extracts purport to be made entirely of malted barley, some are adulterated with such additives as glucose and caramel coloring. Experiment with different brands until you find the few that deliver consistent results.
Amber syrup	1.040	10–18	See above.
Dark syrup	1.040	35–65	See above.
Pale DME	1.047	4–8	See above.
Amber DME	1.047	10–35	See above.
Dark DME	1.047	45–100	See above.

TABLE 3: ADJUNCT AND SUGAR PROFILES

Adjuncts are sources of sugar that are not malted barley, which can be used, in small quantities, to influence the character of your homebrew in many ways.

Adjunct	SG	SRM	Description
Flaked barley	1.028–1.034	1–3	Small additions add flavor and body to dark beers. Mash along with other grains.
Flaked corn	1.035–1.039	0	Often used in large amounts by breweries that wish to add potency and cut costs. Small amounts may add character to lighter beer, but flaked corn must be partial-mashed with an enzyme-rich pale malt.
Flaked oats	1.030–1.035	2–3	Used in oatmeal stout and Belgian witbier. Small amounts impart a smooth mouth feel, enhance body, add a grainy flavor, and aid in head retention.
Flaked rice	1.037–1.039	0	Adds potency to light beers, but imparts little else.
Flaked rye	1.032–1.036	1–3	Rye imparts a dry flavor to beer that is distinct and pronounced. Some people love the taste, but it's not for everyone.
Flaked wheat	1.030–1.036	1–2	Can be used in Belgian wheat beers for added acidity. Small amounts also aid in head retention. Partial-mash with a well modified malt.

Sugars can be used to condition beer, lighten body and flavor, or add character to certain styles of beer.

Sugar	Description
Cane sugar	Used to boost potency and lighten color. Not recommended.
Corn sugar	Essentially glucose. Used mainly as a priming agent for conditioning.
Candi sugar	Used in many strong Belgian beers to lighten body.
Invert sugar	Used in many Belgian beers to boost potency.
Honey	Used to lighten color and body. Also used to make mead.
Treacle	Sometimes used to flavor stouts.
Turbinado	Small amounts used in some pale ales and strong ales.
Molasses	Similar to treacle, sometimes used in darker beers.
Milk sugar	Derived from milk, milk sugar is lactose, an unfermentable sugar used to sweeten stouts.

TABLE 4: HOP PROFILES

The following hops are primarily used as bittering hops. These should be boiled for a minimum of 20 minutes to extract the alpha resins.

Variety	Origin	AA%	Storability	Description
Admiral	Britain	11–14	Fair	Similar to target, but higher in alpha acids.
Bramling Cross	Britain	5–7	Fair	Imparts an earthy, berryish character. Good in darker beers.

Variety	Origin	AA%	Storability	Description
Brewer's Gold	Germany, US	7–10	Poor	Popular bittering hops can be used in many ale recipes. Especially suited for dark. Heavy ales and lagers.
Chinook	US	11–14	Good	Very bitter and pungent. Used primarily for porters and stouts.
Cluster	US	5.5–9	Very good	Very popular in the US, this mild bittering hop has a unique aroma that some people like.
Eroica	US	10–13	Fair	Very bitter hop, used in many beers of medium to high gravity.
Galena	US	10–14	Very good	Versatile and potent, this hop is popular with British and American brewers.
Green Bullet	New Zealand	10–11	Good	Used primarily in Australian lagers. Very bitter!
Northern Brewer	Germany, Britain	7–10	Good	Used in California common beers, German lagers, and British ales. Northern Brewer is pungent, assertive, and bitter.
Nugget	US	10–14	Good	A little goes a long way. This super-alpha hop is very bitter and aromatic. Used in many styles of beer.
Pride of Ringwood	Australia	7–10	Fair	Popular bittering hop in Australia, this hybrid bittering hop is growing in popularity.
Target	Britain	10–13	Poor	Widely used in Britain as a bittering hop.
Zenith	Britain	8–10	Good	Relatively new hop, developed in Britain. Bitter, with some aroma.

Dual hops can be used as bittering agents, and contain the essential oils needed to provide flavor and aroma. These can be introduced throughout the boil.

Variety	Origin	AA%	Storage	Description
Bullion	Britain, US	6–10	Poor	Bitter, but with pungent, spicy aroma and flavor.
Centennial	US	9–11	Fair	Strong bittering hop with Cascade-like aroma and flavor.
Challenger	Britain	7–9.5	Poor	Used in British and Belgian ales for bittering. However, homebrewers are discovering its aromatic qualities. Rare in the US.
Chinook	US	11–14	Good	Versatile hop that can give sweetly fruity citrus character if used late. Good bittering and flavor too.
Citra	US	11–14	Good	Pungent and versatile hop that gives a pronounced citrusy flavor and aroma.
Columbus	US	12–15.5	Fair	The high end of dual hops. Great for bittering and aroma. Used in American pale ales, stouts, and porters.
Hallertauer	Germany	3.5–6.5	Poor	Clean bittering hops with a soft, spicy flavor. Popular and versatile.

Variety	Origin	AA%	Storage	Description
Nelson Sauvin	New Zealand	11–13.5	Poor	Intensely fruity hop, giving a pronounced passionfruit aroma.
Northdown	Britain	7.5–10	Good	Good bittering, flavor, and aroma hop.
Perle	Germany, US	6–9.5	Good	Similar to Hallertauer, this is used as both a bittering and aromatic hop. Used in German lagers and Canadian lagers.
Spalter	Germany, US	3.5–5	Fair	Very refined hop flavor and aroma. Popular as a replacement to super-alpha bittering hops, because of its clean finish. Just use more.
Spalter Select	Germany	4–6	Good	Newer, heartier form of Spalter. Used for bittering and aroma.
Styrian Goldings	Slovenia	5–7	Fair	Fairly neutral finish, a good aromatic for styles that require a soft bouquet. Popular in lagers, Marzen, and some Belgian ales.
Tettnanger	Germany, US	3–5.5	Poor	Floral, spicy aroma, used in wheat ales and many lagers.

Finishing hops are generally low in alpha acids and high in essential oils. Since the oils dissipate quickly, they should be introduced late into the boil, steeped after the boil, or dry hopped.

Variety	Origin	AA%	Storage	Description
Cascade	US	4-7	Poor	Immensely popular aroma hops in the US. Widely used in American pale ales and IPAs. Floral, citrusy aroma and flavor.
Crystal	US	2-5	Poor	Recently developed, resembles Hallertauer.
Fuggles	Britain, US	4-6	Poor	Distinctive British flavor. Crowns British pales, porters, and stouts.
Golding	US, Canada, Britain	3-5	Fair	Classic British hop with a distinctive flavor and aroma. Used in lighter ales.
Kent Golding	Britain	4-6	Poor	Quintessential English flavoring hop. Refined spicy bouquet and aroma. Used in many quality British beers.
Liberty	US	3.5-5	Poor	New variety, similar to Hallertauer, but spicier. Used in German lagers and American ales.
Mt Hood	US	3-5.5	Poor	Another fine outgrowth of the legendary Hallertauer hop.
Saaz	Czech Republic	3.5-6	Poor	Famous Czech hop used in classic Pilsners for its fine, spicy aroma and flavor. Also used in Belgian wheat ales.
Strissel Spalt	France	3-5	Fair	Used in many continental beers, famous in the rural Bière de Garde.
Ultra	US	2-3.5	Fair	New, disease-resistant hop, similar to Saaz.
Willamette	US	4-6	Fair	An American northwestern finishing hop, similar to, but more potent than, the English Fuggles. A very high-quality and popular hop. Used in a variety of British and American ales.

TABLE 5: GLENN TINSETH'S HOP UTILIZATION TABLE

Decimal alpha-acid utilization vs boil time and wort original gravity.

Boil Time	Original Gravity								
(minutes)	1.030	1.040	1.050	1.060	1.070	1.080	1.090	1.100	1.110
0	0.000	0.000	0.000	0.000	0.000	0.000	0.000	0.000	0.000
3	0.034	0.031	0.029	0.026	0.024	0.022	0.020	0.018	0.017
6	0.065	0.059	0.054	0.049	0.045	0.041	0.038	0.035	0.032
9	0.092	0.084	0.077	0.070	0.064	0.059	0.054	0.049	0.045
12	0.116	0.106	0.097	0.088	0.081	0.074	0.068	0.062	0.056
15	0.137	0.125	0.114	0.105	0.096	0.087	0.080	0.073	0.067
18	0.156	0.142	0.130	0.119	0.109	0.099	0.091	0.083	0.076
21	0.173	0.158	0.144	0.132	0.120	0.110	0.101	0.092	0.084
24	0.187	0.171	0.157	0.143	0.131	0.120	0.109	0.100	0.091
27	0.201	0.183	0.168	0.153	0.140	0.128	0.117	0.107	0.098
30	0.212	0.194	0.177	0.162	0.148	0.135	0.124	0.113	0.103
33	0.223	0.203	0.186	0.170	0.155	0.142	0.130	0.119	0.108
36	0.232	0.212	0.194	0.177	0.162	0.148	0.135	0.124	0.113
39	0.240	0.219	0.200	0.183	0.167	0.153	0.140	0.128	0.117
42	0.247	0.226	0.206	0.189	0.172	0.158	0.144	0.132	0.120
45	0.253	0.232	0.212	0.194	0.177	0.162	0.148	0.135	0.123
48	0.259	0.237	0.216	0.198	0.181	0.165	0.151	0.138	0.126
51	0.264	0.241	0.221	0.202	0.184	0.169	0.154	0.141	0.129
54	0.269	0.246	0.224	0.205	0.188	0.171	0.157	0.143	0.131
57	0.273	0.249	0.228	0.208	0.190	0.174	0.159	0.145	0.133
60	0.276	0.252	0.231	0.211	0.193	0.176	0.161	0.147	0.135
70	0.285	0.261	0.238	0.218	0.199	0.182	0.166	0.152	0.139
80	0.291	0.266	0.243	0.222	0.203	0.186	0.170	0.155	0.142
90	0.295	0.270	0.247	0.226	0.206	0.188	0.172	0.157	0.144
120	0.301	0.275	0.252	0.230	0.210	0.192	0.176	0.161	0.147

TROUBLESHOOTING

This chart details some of the common sources of off flavors and other problems that can flaw your homebrew.

Problem	Reason	Cause(s)	Cure
Buttery, butterscotch flavor	High levels of diacetyl	Diacetyl forms during fermentation, as part of a yeast's natural function.	At the end of fermentation, yeast will break down diacetyl. Allow yeast time at the end of fermentation to finalize this process.
Cidery flavor	Spoiled beer	Wild yeast or bacterial contamination.	Maintain correct sanitation procedures.
Cloudy, hazy appearance	Suspended tannins and/or protein matter	Ground grain husks can cloud beer. Also, slow cooling of the wort discourages protein material from dropping.	Properly crush grains. Quickly cool wort to promote a strong cold break.
"Cooked corn," vegetal flavor and aroma	Dimethyl sulfide (DMS)	DMS occurs in pale malt as part of the malting process, and is released in the brew kettle.	Boil the wort strongly and without a cover on the kettle to drive off DMS.
Dry, puckering taste, astringency	Boiled husk material, fruit skins, or excessive hopping rates	Grains and fruit skins are boiled, releasing tannins. Overhopping can also cause resins to form tannin-like molecules.	Remove grains before the boil. Remove skins from fruit, don't boil fruit—pasteurize at 140°F (60°C) for 25 minutes. Keep hopping rates within reason.
Fruity flavors and aromas	Esters	Alcohols and acids can combine to form esters. To a degree this is inevitable, and even desirable for certain styles of beer. It can and should be controlled in most styles, though.	Use a yeast strain that is appropriate to your style. Oxygenate the wort prior to pitching to promote an efficient, healthy fermentation. Ferment at temperatures recommended for your particular style.

Problem	Reason	Cause(s)	Cure
Green apple or cut grass flavor and aroma	Acetylaldehyde	This is an intermediate compound that is normally converted into ethyl alcohol. Weak yeast or short fermentation can result in the presence of acetylaldehyde.	Choose a fresh, quality yeast strain. Prepare a starter for high-gravity worts. Ferment at appropriate temperatures for the required time.
Hot alcohol flavor, spicy, chemical	Fusel alcohols	Formation of other, longer-chain alcohols that are not broken down.	Use a strong, healthy yeast strain that is suited to your style of beer. Ferment under proper temperatures. Maintain sanitation.
Iron, metallic, "bloodlike" taste	Presence of iron	High iron content in water supply, or use of uncoated metals in brewing.	Make sure your water tastes OK. Use a filter or purchase bottled water. Stick to stainless steel.
Medicinal, band-aid, plastic taste and aroma	Phenols	This class of compounds can be produced by excessive heat during mashing and sparging, oversparging, the use of chlorinated water, and the introduction of wild yeast.	Maintain proper temperatures while partial-mashing. Dechlorinate your water supply, or buy bottled water. Maintain sanitation.
Salty	Overuse of brewing salts	Too many mineral ions in solution.	Know the mineral-ion content of your water before adding excess salts. Also, remember that extracts contain mineral ions.
Sherrylike, wet cardboard, stale, flat, winelike flavors	Oxidation, Trans-2-Nonenal	Oxygen can combine with a host of wort material, causing a list of off flavors. Beers will naturally oxidize as they age.	Don't splash! The only time you want oxygen in your wort is just before you pitch your yeast. Conduct smooth transfers from vessel to vessel. Drink beer fresh.
Skunky, "catty" aroma	Light exposure	Light reacts with compounds in iso-hops, forming the very chemical that protects the skunk.	Use only brown bottles, and store these in a dark place. Guard your carboy against light by putting a dark T-shirt—or a plastic garbage bag with a hole cut out of the bottom—over the carboy.

Problem	Reason	Cause(s)	Cure
Soapy, rancid aroma and flavor	Fatty acids	Compounds usually broken down by healthy fermentation.	Use fresh yeast, correct for your style of beer. Oxygenate the wort at pitching, and prepare a starter if needed.
Sour, tart taste	Organic acids	Formed by intrusive bacteria which metabolize wort material differently than yeast does.	Maintain sanitation.
Sulfury, rotten-egg taste and aroma	Hydrogen sulfide	H2S is often formed in small, unnoticeable quantities. Bacterial infection is usually to blame for excessive (noticeable!) amounts.	Maintain sanitation and fermentation temperatures.
Flat beer	No CO2	Underpriming, lack of suspended yeast for proper conditioning. Caps aren't properly sealed, keg has CO2 leak.	Prime with proper amount. Maintain consistent fermentation temperatures. Check vessels for leaks.
Gushing (foams from bottle)	Too much CO2	Bacterial infection which breaks down unfermentable material. Overpriming. Fermentation wasn't completed.	Maintain sanitation. Prime bottles appropriately. Verify the end of fermentation through careful readings and note-taking.
Poor head retention, or no head formation	Detergent residue. Fat-based oils, soap	Unthorough rinsing of equipment.	Rinse three times! Avoid fat-based cleaners.
Ring around neck	Break material or sign of infection	Poor hot and cold breaks, introduction of bacteria.	Strong rolling boil, quick, clean cool-down, maintain sanitation.
Strands of goo in bottle	Pediococcus	Introduction of bacteria. Yeeeh, toss it!	Maintain sanitation. Don't drool over your wort.

▶A German Beerstein, perfect for enjoying your homebrew in traditional style.

GLOSSARY

Adjunct Any source of sugar used in brewing that is not malted barley.

Ale A class of beer fermented at warm temperatures using *Saccharomyces cerivisiae*.

Alpha acids Soluble hop resin that provides bitterness to beer. Alpha acids are measured as a percentage of the total weight of the hop flower.

Alpha acid units (AAU) A formula used by homebrewers to determine the amount of alpha acids derived from boiling hops. AAU = alpha acid percentage multiplied by the amount of hops used, in ounces.

Alpha amylase A diastatic enzyme in barley that breaks down starches into dextrin chains. See beta amylase.

Attenuation The degree to which yeast converts sugars in wort into ethyl alcohol and carbon dioxide.

Autolysis A process in which yeast cells digest each other after most of the sugars in the wort are metabolized. Causes an unpleasant flavor and aroma. This can be avoided if fermented beer is promptly racked off the yeast sediment.

Barley A cereal grain that has been a main ingredient in beer for nearly 10,000 years.

Beer A fermented beverage made from malt, hops, yeast, and water.

Beta acids Harsh, bitter hop resins that are normally insoluble.

Beta amylase A diastatic enzyme in barley that breaks down dextrins into shorter glucose chains. See alpha amylase.

Brewing liquor Term for water used in brewing.

Chill haze Cloudiness in beer that occurs when residual proteins and tannins coagulate in suspension with a temperature decrease. This can result from improper mashing temperatures, oversparging, and irregularities in the fermentation process.

Cold break The precipitation of proteins that occurs when wort is quickly chilled.

Conditioning The process of adding carbon dioxide to beer by allowing yeast to metabolize a small amount of sugar in a sealed keg or bottle.

Dextrins Unfermentable carbohydrate chains that add body to beer.

◀ A craft beer bar.

Diacetyl A compound formed during fermentation that imparts a little taste and aroma of butter or butterscotch.

Diastatic power A measure of the amount of alpha and beta amylase in a quantity of malt.

Dry hopping The addition of hops to a secondary fermenter.

Esters A class of compounds formed during fermentation, which impart fruity flavors and aromas to beer.

Ethyl alcohol The intoxicating agent in beer.

Fermentation The process by which yeast metabolizes wort sugars and excretes ethyl alcohol and carbon dioxide through anaerobic respiration.

Grist Crushed malt and adjuncts that are mixed with hot water to form a mash.

Hops A member of the bine-growing family, *Humulus lupulus*, which is used in brewing to provide bitterness, flavor, and aroma.

Hot break The precipitation of proteins that occurs when the wort is initially brought to a boil.

Hydrometer An instrument that measures specific gravity, degrees Plato, and alcohol by volume in wort and beer.

International bittering units (IBUs) The measure of bitterness in beer based on parts per million of dissolved isoalpha acids in 2 pints (1 liter) of beer.

Isomerization Rearrangement of atoms in a compound. In brewing, the rearrangement of alpha acids into soluble isomers brought on by boiling.

Krausen The thick, foamy head that forms during the early stages of fermentation.

Lager A class of beer fermented at cool temperatures using *Saccharomyces pastorianus*. Also, the process of storing fermenting beer at cold temperatures to produce lager.

Lautering Process of separating wort from the spent grains after mashing.

Lees Yeast sediment that is removed from fermented wort for use in future batches of beer.

Lovibond An old (but widely used) color scale for malt.

Malt Any grain that has been modified for use in brewing, typically barley.

Mash The mixture of hot water and grist. Also, the act of converting malt starches into sugars by exposing the crushed grains to hot water.

Mineral salts Dissolved compounds in water that aid in the brewing process.

Modification The changes in a grain that occur during germination.

Oxidation The negative reaction between oxygen and various components in wort and beer that results in stale or "wet cardboard"-like flavors.

Oxygenation The process of adding oxygen to cool wort to aid in the growth cycle of yeast.

Priming The act of adding sugar before bottling or kegging to produce carbonation.

Racking Transferring wort or beer from one vessel to another.

Reinheitsgebot The German purity law of 1516, which allows only malt, hops, water, and yeast to be used in brewing.

Sanitation The use of certain chemicals to remove microorganisms from clean brewing equipment.

Secondary fermenter A sealed vessel used to mature beer after primary fermentation.

Slurry A semi-liquid solution and yeast and water.

Sparging The act of rinsing surplus sugars from spent grains by sprinkling hot water over the grain bed.

Specific gravity The measure of wort density at a given time. Original gravity is the density of wort prior to pitching. Final gravity is the density of beer after fermentation.

Standard reference method (SRM) A system used to measure the color of beer.

Tannins Compounds derived from a grain husk that can cause haze and astringency in the finished beer.

Trub The protein sediment in wort that forms after the hot and cold breaks.

Wort The sweet, dense mixture of dextrins, sugars, and hops material prior to fermentation.

Yeast A single-celled fungus that changes wort into beer through fermentation.

BIBLIOGRAPHY

BOOKS

Burch, Byron, *Brewing Quality Beers: The Home Brewer's Essential Guidebook*, second edition (Fulton, CA: Joby Books, 1994).

Daniels, Ray, *Designing Great Beers: The Ultimate Guide to Brewing Classic Beer Styles* (Boulder, CO: Brewers Publications, 1996).

Fix, George, *Principles of Brewing Science* (Boulder, CO: Brewers Publications, 1989).

Garetz, Mark, *Using Hops: The Complete Guide to Hops for the Craft Brewer* (Danville, CA: HopTech, 1994).

Jackson, Michael, *Michael Jackon's Beer Companion*, second edition (Philadelphia, PA: Running Press, 1997).

Janson, Lee, B*rew Chem 101* (Pownal, VT: Story Publishing, 1996).

Line, Dave, *The Big Book of Brewing* (Andover, UK: Amateur Winemaker Publications Ltd, 1979).

Lutzen Karl F. and Mark Stevens, *Brew Ware: How to Find, Adapt & Build Homebrewing Equipment* (Pownal, VT: Story Pubishing, 1996).

Mares, William. *Making Beer*, revised edition (New York, NY: Alfred A. Knopf, Inc. & Toronto, Canada: Random House of Canada, Ltd, 1994).

Miller, Dave, *Dave Miller's Homebrewing Guide* (Pownal, VT: Story Publishing, 1995).

Mosher, Randy, *The Brewer's Companion* (Seattle, WA: Alephenalia Publications, 1995).

Owens, Bill, *How to Build a Small Brewery: Draft Beer in Ten Days*, third edition (Ann Arbor, MI: G.W. Kent, Inc, 1992).

Papazian, Charlie, *The Home Brewer's Companion* (New York, NY: Avon Books, 1994).

Papazian, Charlie, *The New Complete Joy of Homebrewing* (New York, NY: Avon Books, 1984).

Smith, Gregg, *The Beer Enthusiast's Guide* (Pownal, VT: Story Publishing, 1994).

Snyder, Stephen, *The Beer Companion* (New York, NY: Simon & Schuster, 1996).

Snyder, Stephen, *The Brewmaster's Bible* (New York, NK: HarperCollins Publishers, Inc., 1997).

PERIODICALS

Bach, Ron, "02 for your Brew," *Southern Draft Brew News*, vol. 4, no. 3 (February/March 1997).

Eames, Alan D., "Beer, Women, and History," *Yankee Brew News* (Summer 1993).

Eckhardt, Fred, "The Joy of Lupulin," *All About Beer*, vol. 17, no. 2 (May 1996).

Ensminger, Peter A., "The History and Brewing Methods of Pilsner Urquell," *Brewing Techniques* (May/August 1997).

Garetz, Mark, "Dry Hopping for Great Aroma," *Brew Your Own*, vol. 3, no. 8 (August 1997).

Jackson, Michael, "Bavarian Wheat Beers— An Accompaniment to Summer," *What's Brewing*, vol. 1, no. 1 (July 1996).

Jackson, Michael. "The True Meaning of Bock," *What's Brewing*, vol. 2, no. 1 (Winter 1997).

Jankowski, Ben. "The Making of Prohibition—Part 1: The History of Political and Social Forces at Work for Prohibition in America," *Brewing Techniques* (November/ December 1994).

Kavanagh, Thomas W., "Archaeological Parameters for the Beginnings of Beer," *Brewing Techniques* (September/October 1994).

Lees, Graham. "The History of CAMRA," *All About Beer*, vol. 18, no. 3 (July 1997).

Lodahl, Martin. "Malt Extracts: Cause for Caution," *Brewing Techniques* (September/ October 1993).

Manning, Martin P., "Airing Things Out: Aeration vs. Oxygenation vs. Oxidation," *Zymurgy*, vol. 19, no. 5 (Winter 1996).

Manning, Martin P., "Recipe Formulation Calculations for Brewers," *Brewing Techniques* (January/February 1994).

Manning, Martin P., "Understanding Specific Gravity and Extract," *Brewing Techniques* (September/October 1993).

Mosher, Randy, "A Turn-of-the-Century British Account of Selected 19th Century Belgian Brewing Methods," B*rewing Techniques* (November/December 1994).

Rabin, Dan, "Secrets of Pitching," *Zymurgy*, vol. 21, no. 2 (Summer 1998).

ACKNOWLEDGMENTS

I couldn't have written this book without help and so I'd like to express my appreciation to those who gave their time, expertise, and support during the various stages of this book. Without exception, the people I met and sought counsel from have been enthusiastic and generous.

First, I'd like to thank Scott Youmans and all the guys at Pinehurst Brewery for giving up time and space for countless questions about professional brewing. Stephen Snyder helped me get this book published and gave me valuable guidance whenever I needed it. I also want to thank all of the folks at American Brewmaster who let me barge in to borrow equipment, take photographs, and solicit advice.

Glenn Tinseth generously allowed me to use his hops charts and formulas for the book. Chris Russell of New York Homebrew and Lynne O'Conner of St. Patrick's of Texas Brewing Supply both gave advice and homebrew recipes. Other recipe contributors include Peter A'Hearn from the Homebrew Mart, Marci from Maui Home Brew Supply, Jim McHale and Lisa Budduck from Beer Unlimited, Jim Tesch from Double Springs Homebrew Supply, and the folks at Alfred's Brewing Supply.

Thanks also to photographer Keith Waterton for his brilliance, perseverance, and wicked sense of humor. Also, to Clare Hubbard, Diana Steedman and Richard Dewing.

Credit must also go to the founding fathers of our beery obsession: Charlie Papazian, Byron Burch, Dave Miller, Randy Mosher, and Ray Daniels. If there was a Mount Rushmore for homebrewing, these guys would be on it.

I also want to thank those who supported me in this endeavor. This includes my wife, Jacqueline, my mom and dad, my sister Kristen and my best brewing bud, David Tuthill. Finally, thanks to my brother, Tom, for introducing me to all this crazy homebrewing stuff in the first place. Next one's on me, Tom.

This book is dedicated to my grandmother. Nana: here's the one book you've yet to read, about the only craft you've never tried

ABOUT THE AUTHOR

Brian Kunath is a professional writer and homebrewer who has been making his own beer since before the Internet was a thing. His rule, to either write about beer or to write while thinking about beer, has served him well in his career. He's worked as a journalist, a managing editor, a copywriter, and a creative director on Madison Avenue. Today, Brian splits his time between New York City and his country home in Woodstock, NY, where he lives with his wife Jacqueline and their Labrador Retriever, Amity. He's currently plotting his next book. Hint: It will be beer-related.

INDEX